William Page Roberts

Liberalism in Religion

And Other Sermons

William Page Roberts

Liberalism in Religion
And Other Sermons

ISBN/EAN: 9783337160296

Printed in Europe, USA, Canada, Australia, Japan

Cover: Foto ©Lupo / pixelio.de

More available books at **www.hansebooks.com**

LIBERALISM IN RELIGION

LIBERALISM IN RELIGION

AND OTHER SERMONS

BY

W. PAGE ROBERTS, M.A.

MINISTER OF S. PETER'S, VERE STREET, LONDON; FORMERLY VICAR OF EYE, SUFFOLK
AUTHOR OF 'LAW AND GOD' 'REASONABLE SERVICE' ETC.

'But what more oft, in nations grown corrupt
And by their vices brought to servitude,
Than to love bondage more than liberty—
Bondage with ease than strenuous liberty—
And to despise, or envy, or suspect
Whom God hath of His special favour raised
As their deliverer? If he aught begin,
How frequent to desert him, and at last
To heap ingratitude on worthiest deeds!'
Samson Agonistes

LONDON
SMITH, ELDER, & CO., 15 WATERLOO PLACE
1886

TO
MY WIFE
CONSTANT COMPANION AND BEST FRIEND

I

DEDICATE THIS VOLUME

PREFACE.

THE words Liberal and Liberalism at once arouse a spirit of mistrust in many minds, which become unsympathetic, irreceptive, and resentful. Even those who appropriate these words in politics are less ready to adopt them in religion. Indeed, it seems as though men had but a strictly limited quantity of mental motor energy, and that those who expend it in one kind of movement have none left for any other. Certainly the sects which are supposed to be the backbone of political Liberalism are the most obstinately immovable in religion; and men ever ready to catch the first breeze impelling to political change have remained stolid as stone to the impulses of spiritual progress. Like Lot's wife, their eyes are fixed on the past, and they cannot stir. But the title I have given to these Sermons carries with it no political connotation. I did not invent it. It is used to denote a party which exists in the Protestant Churches, and which has ever had its analogue in the Church Catholic. Its apostle is St. Paul, and the Church which is without it must have the same fate as the Church of Jerusalem. I should have preferred to speak of the methods of Divine education, or of the dynamics of religion; but I must take the name which foes have given. Of this, however, I am certain, that Liberalism *in* religion is Conservatism *of* religion. If it were not I would not be its apologist. Should this little volume be found useful, I may offer another, intended to show how admirably the Church's Offices of Common Prayer and of the Holy Communion serve to express the worship of a Liberal in religion. The Prayer-Book is for us as well as for our brethren. If in some of its phrases we find simpler meanings — meanings which we think are closer to reality—than the more technical meanings given to them by High or by Low Churchmen, it is none the less dear to us. We do not say to the Ritualist, Go to Rome, or, Go to prison; nor do we declare that the Evangelical ought to become a Dissenter. If I may say so without levity, we are 'Liberal Unionists,' and the Prayer-Book is the bond which binds us all together. Its voice is, 'Ye are brethren ... see that ye fall not out by the way.' I may add that the spirit which should animate Liberalism in religion, and the methods it should pursue, are admirably indicated by Dr. Swainson in his invaluable book on the Creeds. He would scarcely care to be called a Liberal in religion, but his words may be laid down as a rule for our proceedings :—

The fact that religion is a science is very often overlooked; and one consequence is that we hear far too frequently of the opposition between science and theology. But theology is a science; in the common consent of all intelligent believers, it has been made into one. Like geology and astronomy, and history and moral philosophy (mental science), it has its peculiar region of facts and phenomena, its peculiar data, its own principles; but it is a serious mistake on the part of its advocates to conceive and represent that the laws which are to govern our investigations regarding it are of a character totally different from those which govern our investigations into other sciences. It must be recognised that this is a mistake before we can hope to draw generally the intelligence of mankind or even devote ourselves in the spirit of St. Paul to the study of Christianity. Of course I know that there is much of ψευδώνυμος γνῶσις in many of the so-called scientific men of the day, as there is in many of the so-called theologians; and I am not surprised that the chief attacks on the false knowledge of the one party proceed from those who pride themselves most on what is really a false knowledge in regard to the other series of subjects.

THE LIBERAL DEVISETH LIBERAL THINGS, AND BY LIBERAL THINGS SHALL HE STAND.—*Isaiah* xxxii. 8.

Brynygwin-Ucha, Dolgelly:
September 1886.

CONTENTS.

		PAGE
	FREDERICK DENISON MAURICE	1

SERMON

I.	SCEPTICISM	17
II.	REVELATION—I.	28
III.	REVELATION—II.	39
IV.	LIBERALISM IN RELIGION—I.	51
V.	LIBERALISM IN RELIGION—II.	64
VI.	DOES IT MATTER WHAT A MAN BELIEVES?	75
VII.	COMMONPLACE BELIEF IN GOD—I.	89
VIII.	COMMONPLACE BELIEF IN GOD—II.	101
IX.	SHAM IMMORTALITY	112
X.	ETERNAL PUNISHMENT	123
XI.	NEED OF SALVATION	137
XII.	MEANS OF SALVATION	147
XIII.	SPIRITUAL DEPRESSION	157
XIV.	'DEVOTIONALITY'	168
XV.	THE CALLS OF GOD	178

FREDERICK DENISON MAURICE.

S. Peter's, Vere Street, Sunday, February 4, 1883.

To-day there is placed in this Church, by the piety of disciples and wrought by one 'endowed with highest gifts, the vision and the faculty divine,' a memorial to him who from its pulpit taught the Church at large.[1] It is the only monument to any of her ministers which this church possesses; and this will not surprise those for whom the name of Mr. Maurice alone reclaims it from obscurity. But it surprises me, indeed it saddens me. For the bond which unites the minister and the members of his congregation in this church is more than usually close. No parochial obligation constrains them; no what I may call organic cohesion holds them together. Gathered from far and wide by a kind of natural selection, it is to the minister rather than to the church or to each other they are attached. Some sympathy or mental similitude or spiritual affinity draws them to him. Not for long does the minister address himself to reluctant or repellent hearers. No voice of duty bids them endure when

[1] An altar-piece painted by Mr. Burne Jones.

dislike to the minister makes worship difficult. The Church, like the world, is wide, and he is wise who turns from the house of unrest and seeks a sure dwelling and a quiet resting-place. And here congregations have gathered around teachers in times past, held by the bonds of which I have spoken, and teachers and congregations are gone and have left no memorial.

I think it strange that as yet my immediate predecessor, Dr. Coghlan, is unrecorded in this church.[1] He was a man of more than usual intellectual eminence. Many distinguished in the world of mind as well as highly placed in society gave him admiring attention, and in those whom he found congenial he stirred a deep affection. I do not think of comparing any of my predecessors, however distinguished, with Mr. Maurice. Not often does God give one such man in a century, and this century has been highly favoured, for it has had two. But smaller men and men of another rank in life may yet be worthy of affection and remembrance; and the suggestion is chilling, to those whose ambition is to be loved if they dare not look to be venerated, that the attachment of their flock is but a strand of snow, or, to use the words of Burke, ' a largess of inconstancy.' But his claims to be remembered, to whom our monument this day is raised, the whole Church recognises. Only one other Churchman in this century can be placed by his side as an equal.

[1] Since this sermon was preached a monumental brass has been placed in the church to the memory of Dr. Coghlan.

Maurice and Newman have had more shaping and controlling power over the mind of English Christianity than any other teachers the Church, this age, has produced. I have been honoured by the notice of one of them; and he who has once felt the fascination of Newman will keep its charm until he dies. But of the two, I venture to think that the influence of Maurice has been profounder, as it has been more far-reaching, and cannot but be more lasting.

I am afraid that many of the younger generation know little of this great Doctor and Saint of our Church, that they do not read his books or know much what manner of man he was. Those who knew him, and sat at his feet, and caught somewhat of his spirit, and watched his influence circling in ever-wider sweeps, may feel impatient as I speak of their master. They must see how inadequate are the conceptions of him formed by one who never looked upon his face, nor heard the voice whose tones still make sad music in their ears. I ask their forbearance and their sympathy; and towards those of this congregation, once so highly favoured, who now accept such ministrations as I am able to supply, I am moved by a grateful affection. But I am not therefore absolved from speaking to them the truth as it is given to me. I dare not hide it, and least of all when the thought of their great teacher is with me. And it is for them to beware lest they be puffed up with a sense of their own finer perceptions and higher knowledge; lest a subtle Gnosticism diffuse itself as an evil spirit through their minds, making them look down from a height of cold superiority on those who cannot reach the thoughts which they have grasped; and lest the narrow spirit of sect, so hateful to him they venerate, destroy in them the understanding which is given to sympathy.

But the younger generation, who knew him not, or rather who think they know him not, ask, How is it that he is not more spoken of? If he was so great, how was it that he was only minister of this little church, that other men became canons and bishops and decorated chaplains, while the greatest son of the Church was left out, uninvited by place and preferment? One of his most devoted friends,[1] complaining that 'the first theologian' of the day, who had done more 'to widen and deepen English thought than any other,' had been entirely ignored by the dispensers of Church patronage, says, 'Mr. Maurice was not of the stuff of which dignitaries are made;' and adds, 'It is a rare chance in Church government which lands prophets or apostles in stalls or thrones.' It was natural that irritation should stir the minds of those who felt the greatness of their master, when they saw small men raised to great place. But it may have been right and best. It is with regret we see a great scholar taken away from the work which he alone can do for the whole Church, and employed in labours which

[1] Mr. Thomas Hughes.

other men can do as well, it may be better than he. And if this is true of the great scholar, still more is it true of the prophet. The prophet is not in his place of power when his energies are exhausted by incessant administrative toil. He sees so far into the future, and tells such strange things, that the common mass of priests and people do not understand him ; they may be fascinated or frightened, but he is a puzzle rather than a refuge of rest, and whether he be of heaven or of men they cannot tell—indeed they are not quite sure that he may not be of the Devil. We need not regret that fading honours were given to those whose names are now forgotten. The honours of the greatest men are posthumous, and to them is given a crown ' incorruptible and undefiled and that fadeth not away.'

I said that many of the younger generation would confess that they know little or nothing of Mr. Maurice; and yet his hand has given shape to their minds. Inside the Church and outside it men have absorbed his teachings, and are ruled by them, and almost regard them as self-evident, who know not by whom God gave them. He has revolutionised religious thought by his silent, ever-working influence. The change which has come over the tone and temper and intelligence of religious teaching, during the last quarter of a century, is something marvellous. Men seem now to be dealing with reality, while in the past they seemed to be dealing in damaged and worn-out scholastic phrases. When the Florentines saw the statue of David, which Michel Angelo had hewn out of the deformed marble with which they had been so long familiar, they said, 'A dead body has been raised to life.' And when we look at the lifeless forms in which Christian truth used to be presented, and now listen to the Gospel message in churches and chapels where even much may offend us, we cannot keep from saying that 'a dead body has been raised to life.'

Perhaps I should be wrong if I claimed for Mr. Maurice the highest place of scholarship in its technical sense; but his wealth of learning was vast. Even Mr. Mill, who thought his intellectual powers wasted, candidly admitted that 'few men had so much to waste.' Everything he touched he enriched. Where ordinary men saw little, or only that which was commonplace, and where deeper thinkers saw inconsequence or contradiction, he saw an explaining truth, something which shed a light in the deep recesses of his soul, an eternal principle, a message of redemption. To him nothing *real* was commonplace, all was rich and wonderful and vocal, because in all was that which is Divine. 'Every fact in nature,' he said, 'became a fact of humanity, a fact of divinity.' Some may think that often he gave the riches he seemed to discover, that he himself sowed the pearls he so delighted to gather. I admit that his mind was of the richest, unconsciously pouring upon all it touched its affluent wealth. But he was more than rich, he was original; not merely prodigal, he was prophetic. And here he differed from the great man with whom I have compared him. Newman was a priest, but Maurice was a prophet. Maurice saw farther into things than other people, he saw them in vaster relations than other people. That which he saw was often more than they could see. He climbed high, and saw visions beyond of new ranges of truth flooded with the radiance of heaven; and when he called from his lofty station to the peasant minds which never gazed beyond the valley, that there were mountains great and grand which reached unto heaven, some said he was a dreamer and a mystic, and some denounced him as a heretic.

That is a sad story, but heaven has now shed its light upon it. I should not refer to it were it not that that harsh taunt of *heretic* is still flung heartlessly about by people who ought to know better. But even such wise and temperate men as the late Dr. Mozley, Regius Professor of Divinity in the University of Oxford, who himself names Mr. Maurice 'a prophet,' said of one of his writings, 'Many statements and arguments in the chapter appear to us not only highly dangerous, but positively unsound and opposed to the doctrine of the Atonement as revealed in Scripture and always understood in the Church.' In another place, dealing with Mr. Maurice's interpretation of the word Eternal, he describes it as 'an interpretation of Scripture which wholly unsettled, if it did not overthrow, the powerful sanctions of religion contained in the doctrine of Eternal Punishment.' But these teachings of Maurice on the Atonement, and his great faith in God and immortality, which so disturbed the sober Oxford divine, have entered into all forms of English Christianity and sweetened them with the love of God. It has been said that Newman was hounded out of the Church of England. I could not believe such a thing. Bigotry mightier than Newman! Impossible! Newman could never have stayed in the Church of England. If her embrace had been ever so much extended he could not have stayed. It was not a wider Church he wanted. The Church of his birth was too wide already. The great world alarmed him, and he took sanctuary in the Roman Communion. He could not have stayed in the Church of England, and Maurice could hardly have been got out of it. Maurice had been called to enlarge her borders and make her wide as the love of God. He looked into the world with reverence and saw the kingdom of Christ, and said, 'The earth is the Lord's and the fulness thereof.' The one was a cloister mind and the other the spirit of perfect freedom.

That the Church of England is as strong this day as she is, or, better still, let me say, that Christianity has such firm hold on the minds of thinking men and women, is due to such men as Mr. Maurice. The Church of Rome has no place for them, and so infidelity, like a desert, encloses her on every side and ever extends its arid reach. To the Church of England they have been given, and as yet she has not been able to reject them. It is little to say that, even on the subjects with which Mr. Maurice has dealt—and there are few Biblical subjects which he has not treated —he has left many difficulties showing the same defiant front. He himself would have been the very first to admit it. What he cared to reveal was the truth which could save men's lives. He felt that they might stand staring at difficulties until they were too blinded to see God. I think in his eagerness to tell men saving truths, he failed to see some of the difficulties which challenged commoner minds. Mr. Hutton says, 'Maurice's mind was not given to appreciate historical difficulties.' When the great truth was extracted and held up to light, he went on his way, singing his Te Deum, with eyes fixed on heaven. Scepticism and materialism had no place in him. How could they, for he was like Stephen, full of faith and of the Holy Ghost. He believed that the spirit of truth was still guiding men into all truth. Not to find falsehoods and stir unbelief, but to search for the saving truth and proclaim it was his high office.

Alas! may not some of us, who look upon him as a master, have given colour to the reproaches so unjustly directed against him—may not we be finders of fable rather than finders of truth? In one of those simple Gospel explanations which occupy so large a place in his unaffected, unpretentious teaching—a teaching inlaid with large pieces of the Bible, which the reader is inclined to skip, although he says he believes the Bible is the Word of God,—but which at times blaze out with a sudden revealing light, there is a meaning evoked from the parable of the Unjust Steward which should make us ask ourselves, Are we indeed of the truth? The Unjust Steward is he who tells his master's debtors that they owe less than they really do. 'Write fourscore,' says the Unjust Steward, instead of a hundred. And Mr. Maurice says that the Jews won friends among the heathen 'by lowering the standard which they had already by substituting an easy atheism for a restless idolatry.' And I will say, is it not possible that we have been pandering to what we may think the modern spirit and the requirements of the day? We have not been asking for a spirit to guide us into all truth, but listening to a serpent spirit which says there is not much truth at all, and if there is you can never be certain that you have it; which says you need not believe this, and that is not necessary; and to burdened souls who ask are they to subscribe Thirty-nine Articles, reply, Take thy bill and write thirty. Men must turn from us if we have no faith. The scepticism of the pulpit is the seed of infidelity. And what would he say to those who once gathered around him, and called him Master, and heard him tell that it was God who was ruling and redeeming the world, and that only by the word of God may men and States be saved, but who now doubt the possibility of Divine words and see no Divine overruling and recognise no Kingdom of Christ, and say that all is of the earth earthy, and give to fugitive phenomena the name of Positive—

<blockquote>
And yet they know where'er they go
That there hath passed away a glory from the earth.
</blockquote>

Well, he would say with an ancient prophet, 'Cursed be he that trusteth in man and maketh flesh his arm, and whose heart departeth from the Lord.' And yet methinks the curse would be a blessing in disguise, for cursing was ever far from him.

One other man in this century has been named a prophet ; and, like Mr. Maurice, he too bore his witness that 'the things which are seen are temporal and the things which are not seen are eternal.' With him, too, the spiritual was the real. It may possibly be thought that Maurice was not so strong a man as Carlyle, because his words were more temperate. This does not follow. In all Mr. Maurice's writings there are signs of stern self-control. You can feel, as it were, his soul rising within him at times all hot and threatening, and then it is stilled by a strong hand, and the eyes grow calm to see justice and judgment. Explosions of temper and tempestuous words may betray weakness. To cry 'fool' with scornful harshness may be only dyspepsia. I have not told the text to my sermon. Well, here it is—'And the Lord spake unto Moses face to face as a man speaketh unto his friend.' This was the secret of Mr. Maurice's strong self-control. Beneath the eye of God human passions were awed; and tenderness to men, his brethren in the great Brother, chid away resentments, until his foes were embraced and unexpected virtues found in his enemies. Well might Tennyson say of him 'that he was dear to God.'

Time will not allow me to tell of his unceasing labours of practical benevolence. To those who are commonly called the working classes he gave counsel and constant teaching. He did the work to which he invited others. The Home for Destitute Girls, and the Working Men's College, owe their existence to him. The last sermon he ever preached was on this Sunday nine years ago, and then it was for a mission of love. And now I have told those of you who knew him not some of the powers and qualities of one too far above me for complete comprehension. You may find difficulties in your way when you study his writings. He has often been called obscure. I think I have been daring enough to say so myself. But one must live as high a life as he lived if one would enter fully into his spirit. Then possibly the clouds would lie beneath our feet. His natural gifts were of the very highest order, and at their disposition were vast and various treasures of learning. Quick to perceive the finest differences, and subtle in tracking the devious windings of the human heart and mind, pushing behind the shows of things until realities were reached, and inspired by the widest and warmest sympathies so that the shyest truths came forth to meet him, he was a philosopher, a theologian, a philanthropist, and a saint. Various and subtle and rich as Newman, he was more original. Prophet of the Spirit like Carlyle, he knew not how to curse. Pure a saint as Keble, no shadow of religious materialism dimmed his vision of God. What he said of the Emperor Marcus Aurelius I will say of himself: ' Always shunning the display for which so many were eager, not caring to decide about the claims of their different schools, but ready to learn from any of them if they warn him of any insincerity to which he was exposed, or show him a better way than he knew of guiding his character and shaping his actions. Philosophy was never an excuse to him for avoiding troublesome business.' His life was a blessing, and with a blessing he died. I have been told by one [1] who loved him well, and whose medical skill ministered to him in his last hours, that when all seemed over, and the pulse had ceased to flutter and the great repose had begun, strangely the fleeing spirit came back, as though one thing had been omitted, and moved again within its tenement; and raising himself in his bed the saint looked round on those he best loved to see, and with something of his old animation and the voice which can never be forgotten, he said, ' The peace of God which passeth all understanding keep our hearts and minds through Christ Jesus, and the blessing of

[1] Dr. C. B. Radcliffe.

God Almighty, the Father, the Son, and the Holy Ghost, be with us all evermore'—and the blessing done, he died. Can that blessing of peace be lost? It cannot so long as the spirit of him who breathed it animates the Church. Like Christ he knew no will but that of the Father which sent him; and whenever he heard the voice of Christ, whether it called him to work, to suffer, or to die, like her whose form is pictured on that pure monument, he said, 'Rabboni' —my Master.

SERMONS

I.

SCEPTICISM.

'Thy faith hath saved thee.'—*Luke* vii. 50.

THE temper of the present time is sceptical, and it will be more sceptical ere it again becomes faithful. For it will again become faithful. Men drink their cup of unbelief to the dregs before they taste all its bitterness, but it bites them at last. Scepticism cannot be an abiding state; it is a transition stage. 'Scepticism,' says Mr. Carlyle, 'as sorrowful and hateful as we see it, is not an end, but a beginning.' And M. de Tocqueville says, ' Unbelief is an accident, and faith is the only permanent state of mankind.' There is an age of nobler faith before us, and with it of nobler life, or else the world will die. For scepticism is essentially disintegrating, and demoralising, and destroying. Let me tell what I mean by scepticism. People who think in a foggy kind of way, and express themselves accordingly, apply the word sceptic to everybody who does not believe the doctrines which they consider to be fundamental, to any writer or teacher who denies something which they hold to be

C

sacred. It is applied, indiscriminately, to him who cannot conceive the personality of God, or who does not assent to the Deity of Christ, or who questions the traditional authorship of some book of the Bible, or who denies the doctrine of unending sin. But men may do all these things, and yet be men whose fibre and substance is faith. The man who denies one thing or disbelieves one system, may believe most firmly in another; his whole life may be pervaded and ruled by positive convictions and an ardent faith. Such a man cannot be called a sceptic, any more than a Romanist may call a Protestant a sceptic, or a Protestant call a Romanist a sceptic. You may call a man a misbeliever who holds a different faith from yours, and he will equally look upon you as a misbeliever; but a misbeliever is a believer, and not a sceptic.

I have said that scepticism is in its nature and influence demoralising. But I dare not say that Atheism or Agnosticism necessarily leads to immorality, for there need be no scepticism in either of them. I am deeply convinced that real faith in God gives a moral energy and a moral ideal which nothing else can equal; and that if we in any way, as individuals or as nations, lose this energising faith in God, our moral efforts will have a less lofty reach. But if a man have taken something else instead of God—if, for instance, with the Comtists, he have taken Humanity for the object of his worship and service, have taken it in deed and in truth—then his life will be marked by a noble morality.

He cannot have the inspiring emotions of piety—at least I cannot think that he can—but he may be an ardent, unselfish philanthropist. He believes in Humanity; he is no sceptic, and his moral life is saved by faith.

Scepticism is the exact opposite of faith; it is, in a word, faithlessness; it is the state of not believing in anything. Edgar Quinet says, 'Rather than half believe, half love anything, I prefer to believe nothing, love nothing.' Scepticism is believing nothing, loving nothing. In its latest development it is a mode of regarding all spiritual things with indifference or contempt. Scepticism has been taught as a system of philosophy, and applied to the whole realm of knowledge; at times it has seized upon particular provinces of thought; and it has been most hurtful as a generally diffused spirit and temper. There is no call in these days to controvert scepticism as a comprehensive system of philosophy. It must stultify itself. Nor yet need I call your attention to those manifestations of scepticism in the past which for a time mocked religion out of countenance; such, for instance, as prevailed amongst a large section of the educated classes under the empire of the Cæsars, to a certain extent during the Italian Renaissance, and more confessedly in England and France of the eighteenth century. The forms of Voltaire and Gibbon at once rise up before us. The scepticism I am careful to speak about is the scepticism of the present rather than that of the past; not the scepticism outside Christianity, but the scepticism inside Christianity; not the scepticism which leans against the portals of the church, and mocks airily at those who enter—

> And mocking is the fume of little hearts—

but the scepticism which takes seats in church, and bows at the proper place, and is against innovation.

It is impossible to deny that thought is more daringly exercised and expressed in religious matters than it used to be. Views are openly put forth, and without fear of rebuke, both by laymen and clergymen, which would scarcely have been ventured upon a hundred years ago even by those who were suspected of freethinking. Great numbers of people have what are called broader views, more liberal ideas, than were allowed to their fathers. Retaining their connection with religious communities, they yet interpret Christianity in a way different from that of the past. Our popular literature is saturated with the spirit of criticism, and the populace cannot escape its influence. It would ill become me to condemn this new-found liberty. If I am any good in the world, I gathered such strength as I have from the air of freedom. The future of the Church is for the free. With Burke I would say, 'When everything liberal is withheld, and only that which is servile is permitted, it is easy to conceive upon what footing they must be in such a place.' But every great movement and form of life has its dangers. This freer thinking, which men of all religious parties in the Church practise more or less, may be allied with decay of faith and death of piety; perhaps these are its special dangers. And we must watch against the foe; for it were better to be the victim of superstition, if filled with piety towards God, than to be ever so enlightened, with a hard heart.

But practically—and do bear with me if I speak plainly, for it is no good acting the part of Christians if we are not; if we cannot be Christians, at least we may be honest men and say so—is it not true that devotion to God and Christ, amongst large numbers who go to churches and chapels on Sundays, and especially amongst those who hold themselves to be progressive thinkers, is not very fervent and impulsive? Do we really find worship—I do not mean music or preaching—do we find worship a delight? How many of us, *who don't believe ever so many things*, can say with the poet of Evangelicalism, 'Oh for a closer walk with God'? What do we really know of a 'walk with God'? What part in our life has such a saying as this—'My heart and my flesh cry out for the living God'? Where is the man, who thinks that the old doctrines are blunders or at least unnecessary, whose spirit murmurs to itself, 'For me to live is Christ, and to die is gain'? There are emotions of Christian piety which circulate like life-blood through the soul of him who is devout, which make his Church service a strange joy, and his Communion feast a mystic rapture, and send him into the world to seek and to save the lost. There are such emotions. But are they ours? By their fruits shall ye know them. By our fruits must we know ourselves; and if there are duties and observances which we allow to be Christian, if there is a communion which we name divine, and if we neglect those duties, and do not enter into that sacred communion, then we must put it to ourselves that we are paralysed by scepticism.

Now this paralysing temper—for with many of us scepticism is a temper rather than an intellectual canon—is extending and becoming epidemical. It perhaps may be accounted for by the fact that times of creativeness and originality are often followed by times of indifference, of weariness, of collapse—in other words, of scepticism. Evangelicalism and Tractarianism were both creative or recreative movements. Great forces were expended in their accomplishment. Their oppositions and contradictions, and the fierce passions which their conflict provoked, may have done something to bring about a time of weariness, which turns itself away from the distractions of controversy, and will not decide upon any thing—in other words, is sceptical. Practically, as it relates to individuals, it may result from familiarity with denial. The new form of religious method, soon, to show itself in constructive power—for in each age God has a new teaching and lesson—has had in some cases a work of denial to perform. Just as the great Reformation had a work of denial to perform, so must it be with every reformation. But the Reformation had something else to do besides this. It would soon have disappeared if it had only come to tell men that they were not to believe in this and not to believe in that. Religious Nihilism will no more save men's souls than political Nihilism will save the State. We must give men something better than the creed of levity, every article of which begins, 'I don't believe.' 'The affirmative class,' says Emerson, 'monopolises the homage of mankind.' We may have to deny, but it should be that we may more savingly affirm. But getting into the way of denying may establish a habit of denying, until a flippant temper of scepticism is established, which babbles, in juvenile improvidence, of what it does not believe; and is so clever as to dispense with the supernatural and dogmas and —'well, we don't quite know—but all those sorts of things.' Can anything be feebler than that? What does it believe? Men cannot be saved by what they do not believe, any more than a man can be rich in a property he does not possess.

But indolence may result in scepticism no less than familiarity with denial. On the whole, this is rather a weary time, when men cannot take trouble about anything. Look at our popular books, and papers of gossip, and reminiscences, and memoirs. Everything now is done into small summaries, and the great classics are diluted, and made effervescent with the modern spirit, and supplied in the smallest quantities required. Instead of thinking out solemnly the grounds of our faith, and knowing what it is we believe, and why, and resting upon it with the consciousness of reasoned conviction, men acquiesce in a traditional orthodoxy, or subside into a shallow scepticism. Where is the hunger for faith which makes men labour for the food? I can almost agree with the words of Lessing, especially when I remember that in gaining the knowledge of God there may be eternal progress, when he says, 'Not the truth of which a man is or believes himself possessed, but the sincere effort to come behind the truth, makes the worth of the man. For not through the possession, but through the investigation of truth does he develop those energies in which alone consist his growing perfection.' And I am sure that I accept the teaching of the Platonic Socrates in his answer to Menon: 'Some things I have said of which I am not altogether confident. But that we shall be better and braver and less helpless if we think that we ought to inquire than we should if we indulged in the idle fancy that there was no knowing and no use in searching after what we know not—this is a theme upon which I am ready to fight in word and deed to the utmost of my power.'

Again, is not scepticism very often the product of cowardice? Men seem to see where their thoughts will carry them if they dare to inquire, and the prospect alarms them. If they come to such a conclusion, they must give up this, or leave that pleasant place, or make that damaging confession; they must become poor, or neglected, or take up some painful, unrewarded toil. And so they give up thinking, and do not look any more at the attracting, alarming prospect, and persuade themselves that the land they have seen is only a mirage; and yet they know it is real. And is not scepticism very often the attitude in which hopelessness expresses itself? 'Where is thy God?' is the cry of blind despair. There can be little surprise if, as it relates to one part of our great empire, political scepticism should take possession of men's minds. What's the good of trying any more? is likely to be the heart-breaking question of those whose efforts have been baffled again and again. We must shake ourselves up, whatever political party we may be allied with, lest a despairing stupor overwhelm us; and we must watch lest an ungovernable ferocity seize upon us. Scepticism may produce apathy, it may drive into mania. We must steadily keep going on in the direction of justice and generosity, and never cease to work, and never cease to hope. It has been said that 'indolent scepticism combines naturally with political indifferentism.' I will say that hopeless scepticism may end in reckless raving fury.

And thus, as I conclude my sermon, I come back upon the statement with which I started, that scepticism is essentially demoralising. But pray keep in mind what I said or implied, that scepticism does not mean not believing what we believe; does not mean what we may call heresy. The heretic may be a man strong in faith. The object of his faith may not be, in all respects, the same as the object of our faith, but he may be a firm believer. It is scepticism, the unbelieving condition, the faithless state of mind, which is demoralising. Listen to these words of a German philosopher. 'It is as true of the Greek Sophists as of the French Encyclopædists, that the morals, which had grown up with the religious dogmas, were impaired with them; that individualism, sensualism, and a superficial rationalism put an end to all sincere devotion in the search for truth and in the investigation of the moral principles of life, until at last an all-destroying scepticism, a dialectic and rhetoric to which everything was mere sport, threatened to take possession of the popular consciousness.'

Yes, indeed, scepticism is all-destroying because it destroys all energy. A man who has any faith whatever must do something; but he who has no faith can do nothing, and may drift into anything, drift into a bottomless unlighted pit. Let us beware of this numbing, paralysing malady. If we are thinking that we believe certain things and do not do them, then let us suspect that the chill hand of scepticism is touching us, that it may embrace us, and hold us fast —a corpse which takes away our vital heat—until the chills of death are impressed upon us. 'What does it matter?' says scepticism, indolent, pusillanimous, or hopeless. 'What does anything matter?' Well, it matters this—the loss of the soul. Of the tree of scepticism the eternal law of God is, 'In the day thou eatest thereof thou shalt surely die.' All noble ideals and ambitions and possibilities perish in the presence of scepticism. It leaves—

> No God, no heaven, no earth in the void world,
> The wide grey lampless deep unpeopled world.

From such a scepticism as this, good Lord, deliver us.

II.

REVELATION.

I.

'The secret things belong unto the Lord our God; but those things which are revealed belong unto us and to our children for ever, that we may do all the words of this law.'—*Deuteronomy* xxix. 29.

THE long and painful experience of mankind has convinced men that there are things which they cannot explain, mysteries which are insoluble; about which one thing only is clear, that they never can become clear. And this sense of powerlessness, which at times is distressing, affects not only the deep and laborious thinker, but it tortures as well the humblest man and the weary partner of his life. For if the speculative intellect is only given to some, the feelings are the possession of all, and the feelings rise up in their anguish and despairingly ask Why? and there is nothing to answer. The mother whose eyes are fastened on the dead child, the powerful and far-seeing mind unable to do its work because of physical disease, the man whose fortune has been destroyed by the faults of others, the philanthropist appalled at the amount of human misery and sin which no labour seems to diminish—all ask in vain Why? The questions, Why is there any evil if God is good and God is omnipotent? and, How can I be free and responsible if all my future is certain and known to God so that nothing can alter it? and questions like these, which rise up from the poor cradle of the dead babe, and are the despairing perplexity of many an earnest religious inquirer, attest the fact that there are things which, in this life at least, refuse to give up their secret.

And if the long experience of the race tells us that for some things we cannot get explanations, that, whether we are patient or not, the mystery will still stand before us unmoved and unchanging, like the black cruel cliffs which throw back the ever-beating sea, so too declare the materialistic teachers of to-day. These carpenters of science seem to say, there is only one thing you *can* do, and that is cut up the world into positive planks; there is only one thing you can look forward to doing in the future, and that is to doing the same thing, only doing it faster, now by steam, then by electricity, and then perhaps by something else; until knowledge becomes a vast timber yard of regulation planks all positively wooden, with no philosophy, metaphysics, nor theology about them. Yet the materialist, too, is compelled to recognise the existence of that which he cannot reduce, with his saws and planes and chisels, to scientific shape, and he says, Leave the unknowable and stick to the positive. I am disposed to agree with the materialist, only there are things which he calls unknowable which I say are freely offered to our knowledge; things plain in this world, where so much is mysterious, which he says are obscure; and the text recognises alike the spirit of uninquiring reverence and of rational freedom. 'The secret things belong unto the Lord our God; but those things which are revealed belong unto us and to our children for ever, that we may do all the words of this law.'

'But I do not believe that there are any things revealed,' is a likely answer of to-day; 'I do not accept what you call revelation. I accept what Nature teaches me. If Nature teaches a natural religion, I can accept that; but this supernatural revelation, this revelation of mysteries inaccessible to the human reason, for the comprehension of which it is utterly inadequate, this I do not accept. It is the resource of irrational pietism and the justification of fanatical intolerance.' Now such a statement as this calls for consideration. It may be that certain things have been called revelations which are not properly revelations, and that certain ideas have been attached to revelations, or rather regarded as essential parts of all revelations, which need not be so regarded, and which at least are separable in thought from the proper idea of revelation. 'We find every day instances of men resting their faith in a truth on some grounds which we know to be untenable, and we see what a terrible trial it sometimes is when they find out that this is so, and know not as yet on what other grounds they are to take their stand. And some men succumb in the trial and lose their faith together with the argument which supported it. But the truth still stands, in spite of the failure of some to keep their belief in it, and in spite of the impossibility of supporting it by the old arguments.'[1]

Mr. Gladstone has lately told us that 'there is no definition, properly so called, of revelation either contained in Scripture or established by the general and permanent consensus of Christians.' But one would have thought that its meaning was so obvious that for this reason, while the word has ever been freely used in the Church, it has not been defined. To reveal a thing simply means to make it clearly known, so to put forth a truth, a fact, that it is seen for what it is, to bring a thing out of obscurity into daylight. To reveal a thing is to make known something which previously had been altogether hidden or left very much in obscurity. Some years ago Mr. Maurice published a tractate on the use of the word revelation in the New Testament, proving that it means in all cases ' the giving of light or the removal of a veil.' And the late Regius Professor of Divinity in the University of Oxford, Dr. Mozley, in his lectures on miracles, says, ' A revelation is, properly speaking, such only by virtue

[1] Bishop Temple.

of telling us something which we could not know without it.' But if this be the meaning of revelation, 'the giving of light, the removing of a veil'—if indeed it be 'telling us something which we could not know without it'—then, at first sight, there is something quite thoughtless in a man saying he cannot accept revelation. For to say that, would mean he could not accept anything which was made clear to him. Not to accept revealed truths, or the truths of revelation, primarily, can only mean not to accept truths which have been made quite clear, truths held up in the daylight for a man to look at and be sure that they are and what they are. Not to accept revealed truth must mean, not to accept truth which is plain, from which the veil has been removed; and such a state of mind would be one of unreason and mental aberration. And yet men thoughtlessly go on saying they cannot accept revelation. They must certainly mean something else by revelation than that which is made clear, or they could not so stultify themselves.

But I can almost hear the angry rejoinder, 'That is all very well, but it is not to the point. It is quibbling. You have been dealing with the obvious etymology of the word. We mean it in its technical sense. To put it plainly, we do not accept the Bible. There, that is plain.' But I do not think it is quite plain. At any rate, I do not think it is quite sensible. You cannot mean that there is nothing true in the

Bible. You cannot mean that you do not accept the truths of the Bible, for of course all men—characteristically men of science—accept truth from whatever quarter it may come. Not to accept a truth, which is seen to be a truth, is not merely a blamable infidelity, it is, I almost think, a mental impossibility. When it is said by any one that he does not accept the Bible and does not believe in the Bible, he must mean that there are parts which he thinks are not true, or parts which are so mysterious that he cannot understand them. It is quite impossible that he can mean that he puts away from him as worthless or untrue everything contained in the Bible from beginning to end. For instance, when he is told that it is the duty of man to love his neighbour as himself, he would scarcely deny that that is a rule of living which would do much to increase the goodness and happiness of man, a law of well-being clearly expressed, a revelation—an ethical revelation—capable of being verified in human experience. So that the very man who, uncritically and without exactness of mind, says he does not accept the Bible or revelation, must admit, when he thinks of it, that there are at least some things which are true in the Bible, some things which are good, and that these things are clear and plain things—in other words, he must admit that there are Bible revelations, that is, truths which are clearly put forth in the Bible, which he cannot refuse, to which he must submit.

But it is answered, 'We do not reject the plain

and excellent moral teachings which may be found in the Old and New Testaments. What we mean is that we do not accept them because they are written in the Bible, or because they are said to be supernaturally inspired and authenticated by miracles. We accept these excellent moral teachings because they commend themselves to our reason and to the reason of the race; but what we cannot accept are these mysteries, these incomprehensible, unthinkable doctrines which are revealed in the New Testament.' In the next sermon I shall consider the connection between revelation and what we call the supernatural. But to the second objection I reply at once, a mystery is not a revelation. It is the very opposite of a revelation. As long as a thing is a mystery it is not a revelation. As long as a thing is a mystery to any man, so long that thing to him is not a revelation, even when it has become a revelation to more powerful minds. St. Paul always put the two things, mystery and revelation, as direct opposites of each other. It was hidden from the Jewish mind, for instance, that it was the purpose of God to join all mankind together in one religion by the revelation of Christ. That idea did not present itself to the Jewish mind as the clearly seen purpose of Divine Providence; and St. Paul says it was a mystery 'hidden from ages and from generations, but now was revealed by God's Holy Apostles and prophets.' But when it was revealed it ceased to be a mystery; and to talk of a revelation which is at the same time a mystery is a contradiction. You may recognise the fact of a mystery. Mysteries may confront us in the Bible as they do in other books, in the works of science as in the events of human life; but so long as they are mysteries they cannot be called revelations, and our conduct with regard to them may well be guided by our text. In many cases it may well be that of the Agnostic, to leave them alone; or, with the pious soul, to leave them with Him to whom there is no mystery and all is revelation. 'Secret things belong unto the Lord our God, but those things which are revealed belong unto us and to our children, that we may do all the words of this law.'

> Thy throne is darkness in the abyss of light,
> A blaze of glory that forbids the sight.
> O teach me to believe Thee thus conceal'd,
> And search no farther than Thyself reveal'd.[1]

I freely admit that there are mysteries confronting us in the Old and New Testaments. Truths are intimated, suggested, pointed at, dimly outlined, like a mountain castle scarce seen through the mists of evening which fill the valley; but, inasmuch as they are not clear, to that extent they cannot be said to be revealed. They may be the outlines of great facts, suggestions of most certain truths; but until they are brought to light they are not revealed truths. And so I think it may be with some of the theological

[1] Dryden.

doctrines which are said to be revealed in the New Testament. I should say that they are intimated, suggested, hinted at, implicitly contained, it may be, in the New Testament, but not revealed. Some are of such a nature that they cannot be made clear to the human mind. They are beyond us. They are Divine mysteries which it is reverent for us to place with the secret things which belong unto the Lord our God. Why even Dr. Newman declared, at a time when he was insisting on the most dogmatic theological precision in the English Church and was the fierce denouncer of 'Liberalism in religion,' 'that as regards the doctrine of the Trinity the mere text of Scripture is not calculated either to satisfy the intellect or to ascertain the temper of those who profess to accept it as a rule of faith.' It was the theological ages which drew forth the intimations and suggestions of the Bible—in a word, that which it had left as mysteries or dim suggestions—into dogmatic definition.

Let me advise those who have been perplexed and bewildered by some of these subjects, reverently to lay them on one side, and rather to devote themselves to the revelation which it has pleased Almighty God to make, and that is Himself. 'Revelation,' as Mr. Maurice says, 'is always the unveiling of a person.' It is Christ who is the revelation of God, Christ who is the manifestation of the Father, Christ who makes the character of God plain and clear. He is a revelation indeed, for in Him was the fulness of the Godhead bodily. He it was who showed clearly the God of all, intelligible, beneficent, adorable, showed Him thus in His own human unquenchable love and devotion to man. Well might He say, 'He that hath seen Me hath seen the Father.' God the Infinite Spirit is a mystery. God in the face of Jesus Christ, God as redeeming, saving love in the midst of men, is the Word of life which can be seen and handled. 'Look unto Me and be ye saved all the ends of the earth.'

III.

REVELATION.

II.

'The secret things belong unto the Lord our God; but those things which are revealed belong unto us and to our children for ever, that we may do all the words of this law.'—*Deuteronomy* xxix. 29.

THE Bible is not the sole medium of revelation. The Church has been the minister of God in unveiling and drawing forth into dogmatic precision, truths, which have been but dimly suggested in Holy Scripture. But in some cases Churches have fallen into error. It has been recently laid down that 'the Catholic faith and Apostolic order of the Church are unalterable and may not be touched.'[1] Now, if by the 'Catholic faith' be meant the sum of truth, the Mind of God, Eternal Verity which is and which was and which is to come, then we all admit that the Catholic faith is unalterable. But the knowledge of the Catholic faith has never yet been complete and perfect. It has been communicated gradually. The knowledge possessed by Jewish prophets was less than that which Apostles enjoyed. When Christ said to His chosen

[1] Committee of Convocation.

ones, 'I have many things to say unto you, but ye cannot bear them now,' they did not possess the 'Catholic faith' in its fulness. It is perfectly certain that the doctrine of the Divine Trinity was held in clearer definitions and more conscious possession after the first great Councils of the Church than when she had nothing but the letter of Scripture. Cardinal Newman says that Scripture of itself, 'instead of being a source of instruction on the doctrines of the Trinity and Incarnation, was scarcely more than a sealed book, needing an interpretation, amply and powerfully as it served the purpose of proving those doctrines when they were once disclosed.' Bishop Jeremy Taylor says, 'Original sin as it is at this day commonly explicated was not the doctrine of the primitive Church; but when Pelagius had puddled the stream, St. Austin was so angry that he stamped and disturbed it more.' Newman declared 'it had often been shown' that the doctrine of Purgatory was 'no received opinion during the first ages of the Gospel. . . . Hardly one or two short passages of one or two Fathers for six centuries can be brought in its favour, and those, at the most, rather suggesting than teaching it. In truth, the doctrine seems to have occurred to them, as it has been received generally since, first from the supposed *need* of such a provision in the revealed scheme—from (what may be called) its naturalness in the judgment of reason; and next in consequence of the misinterpretation of certain texts.' Hagenbach, in his 'History of Doctrines,' says that 'Protestants and Roman Catholics established the doctrine of Atonement on Anselm's theory of Satisfaction . . . a doctrine established with an amount of ingenuity, and a completeness of reasoning, *hitherto unattained* . . . a doctrine the first contemporaries and first successors of Anselm were far from adopting in all its strictness.' The Lutheran doctrine of Justification by Faith, was something new to the masses of the Christian world, and was condemned by the Council of Trent. 'Formally and literally stated, then, the Lutheran dogma of justification by faith is inconsistent with the first principles of common sense and natural religion, that in this shape no human being can possibly believe it. It requires us to believe that that which makes a man pleasing to God, or justification, has nothing to do with morality or goodness in him; and being moral creatures, we cannot believe this.'[1] The history of the Church bears witness to the gradual way in which the 'Catholic faith' has been given to the mind of man. And if the Christian Church shows us the evolution of dogma, and the variations in dogma, the English Church shows the reversibility of dogma and the reformability of dogma. It has denied some things which the Church had previously affirmed, and corrected other things which the Church had before imperfectly expressed. That was one work of the Reformation, and who shall say it is

[1] Mozley.

now complete? Certainly Holy Scripture does not; for we are led by it to look for a day of *fuller* and *clearer* perceptions of Divine Reality. 'Now we see through a glass *darkly*, but then face to face. Now I know *in part*, but then shall I know even as also I am known.'

But there are those who say they cannot receive a revelation on the ground that it is supernatural, that they only know that which comes through the mind of man, and is capable of justifying itself to the human reason. Now I affirm that the Bible revelations have come through the mind of man. I am not inquiring how they got there; but, however they got there, they were convictions, certainties, in some man's mind, which he declared to his fellows. They have come through the mind of man. They are capable of justifying themselves to the human reason, and these things I shall attempt to prove. But first let me deal with those who decline to accept revelation on the ground that it is supernaturally or miraculously authenticated. Well, then, accept it on the ground that it is plain truth. For remember it is not miracles which make a thing true. They may lead some one to give heed to a statement which is made as a truth, who might have passed it by but for the wonder or miracle; but a thing is not true because of the miracle. 'A miracle,' says Professor Mozley, 'cannot oblige us to accept any doctrine which is contrary to our moral nature or to a fundamental principle of religion.' A thing is true just because it is a fact, a part of the constitution of things, a law of their being. Ten thousand miracles could not make an untruth true, and ten thousand miracles would not make a truth a whit truer. If a thing is true, it makes no difference to its truth whether a child, a scholar, a poet, or philosopher declare it; or whether it be declared by some one who is called an apostle or a prophet, of whom it is said that he healed the blind or cast out devils. A truth of inspiration is no truer than a truth of induction or of demonstration. Truth is simply truth wherever it may come from or however it be communicated.

The Christian revelation offers itself as a guide for a life which reaches from the present into eternity. It tells the way in which the soul may rise superior to evil of every kind, and so it is said that Christ came 'to save His people from their sins.' Now this law of life, this saving method of Christ, is a thing that can be tried. Men can find out by experience whether it can do what it professes to do. Just as you can try a medicine and find out whether or not it is effective, so you can listen to Christ's words and find out whether they are indeed a revelation of salvation. They commend themselves at first sight to nearly all men as laws which are good and high. They can be tried, and it will be found that they are also true and practicable. Take them then on the ground of their truth—for it is not miracles which make them true—and at least prove their saving powers before you enter upon the difficult realm of the supernatural. This was the test to which Christ submitted His revelation. He said, 'If any man will do His will, he shall know of the doctrine whether it be of God or whether I speak of Myself.' What would you think of a man who declined to take a medicine, which had proved by large experience to be efficacious, because it was said to have been whispered, in ancient days, to some one in a dream, or a mysterious being had told it to some mage or medicine-man of the past? The one practical question is, Does it cure? The question, How was the cure discovered? is purely historical; and it is improper, and I think I may say irrational, for a man either to reject or disparage or ignore that which has the appearance of truth, and offers itself for verification in individual experience, simply because the revealer of the truth is said to have been a wonder-worker. Any man can try Christ's method of salvation, and find out for himself whether indeed it is the power of God and the wisdom of God. The humblest man can test it and prove whether it is true or not. But to prove whether or not some miracle took place is a very different thing indeed. One man will conclude that the miracle did take place, another that it may have taken place, and a third that it did not take place. I can never be certain what effect upon an individual mind may be the evidence which I bring before it for the truth of a miracle. I may be convinced of it, but

I can never be certain that the same evidence will convince some one else, indeed I may be very doubtful whether it will or not. But I am sure about Christ's revelation of the plan of salvation, I am certain of its effect when it is honestly tried and faithfully adopted. Its evidence is in itself, and, as Christ said, 'The words that I speak unto you, they are spirit and they are life.' No man is justified in refusing Christ's laws for life and wellbeing on the ground that they are miraculously attested. If they are true, that is their sufficient foundation. And yet even Mr. Carlyle has spoken in a thoughtless way more befitting the flighty readers of superficial magazines. He could not believe in a 'revelation technically so called—a revelation, that is to say, supposed to be established by historical miracles.' But surely he could believe in a revelation—that is, something which was made clear to him. There were revelations made to him, truths which came out clearly in his mind, which vindicated themselves as truths, and which were not proved to be true by scientific methods. He might not be able to tell how they came to him, but they were deep and intense personal convictions which rooted themselves in his mind. His spirit said, 'That is a truth which it were well for men of the world to take hold of.' The revelations which came to Carlyle he communicated to his fellows; telling them, and in no measured language—for he was an uncompromising preacher of damnation—what would take place if they refused to hearken to his words. And men listened and were caught by the asseverations, and they tried them in practice; and some of them have told us that the teaching of Carlyle provided them with a religion. 'Thy own God-created soul,' says Carlyle, ' is a revelation.' But then some other man's ' God-created soul ' may also be a revelation. And if a revelation comes from a man's ' God-created soul,' may it not be told to other men, and produce in them the deep conviction that these things are true ? If thy own soul is a revelation, so may be the soul of some other man who is bigger and better than thou.

Now this truth, enunciated by Carlyle, is overlooked by some men—I mean the truth that the human soul can impart or be the medium of revelations. Modern materialism, which can scarcely be charged with shyness or retiring habits or humbleness of mind, does at times seem to forget that man, the human mind, is the greatest factor in Nature; and that a study of Nature which does not give chief importance to the study of mind, is not the statue but the torso of science. Here are the fine pulpit words of a worshipper of matter : ' The volume of inspiration is the book of Nature, of which the open scroll is ever spread forth before the eyes of man . . . on the earth it is illustrated by all that is magnificent and beautiful, in the heavens its letters are suns and worlds.'[1]

[1] Draper.

But let it not be forgotten that the book of Nature has its chapter on man. If the volume of Nature is the only truly inspired volume, that part of it, the most important part of that volume which we call man, is at least equally inspired; and we must learn what man's nature says as well as what the earth says, and suns and worlds. And as surely as the earth says gravitation, so surely, as a fact of Nature, does the mind of man say God. To refuse to receive revelation while professing to be taught by Nature is to be self-contradictory.

For revelation is one of the facts of Nature, whatever be our theory of it. It is the fact that certain things have come unto the minds of certain men with startling, convincing clearness—as true, unalterably true, eternally true; so true, that they have said that they were the words of the Eternal, taught them by a higher reason than their own. And they have told them to their fellows, who have proved them true by experience. You cannot study Nature and yet pass by a whole series of the facts of Nature. And these revelations are facts of Nature. One man may explain them in one way, and another in another; but the facts of mind are facts of Nature, and if the volume of Nature is an inspired book, so too must that part of it be inspired which we call the mind of man. It is the order of Nature that from time to time great discoveries are made. These are revelations which appear before great men, and are given by them to smaller men. But if we believe in God, then we believe that these revelations are given in accordance with His mind and will; in other words, that they are Divine revelations. All that comes by Divine law, by the constitution framed by the Divine mind, is a Divine work; just as we properly say that each new being born into the world has been created by God.

Thus revelation is natural, and at the same time supernatural. It comes from the mind of man, it comes according to the mind and determination of God. And therefore what is called natural religion is at the same time revealed religion. Coleridge distinctly says, 'I know no religion but revealed.' Mr. Maurice says, 'In place of revealed religion, which is set up to compete with a number of other religions, we shall acknowledge a God who has been revealing Himself at "sundry times and divers manners" to the nations of the earth.' And Dr. Newman says, 'No people (to speak in general terms) has been denied a revelation from God.' But it is not pretended that all the religions of the world have been attended by unusual displays of Divine power, or were miraculously imparted. Somehow, certain truths were borne in upon the minds of some men, and were taught by them, with much, no doubt, that was erroneous, to their fellows. Indeed, Dr. Newman says that 'one difference between our revelation and theirs is that ours is authenticated.' So that he at least admits that revelations may be unauthenticated. I cannot agree to this. They may not be authenticated by miracle, but they are authenticated. Whatever portion of truth was revealed to any nation in times past, authenticated itself. If it was a revelation, it was a truth clear to those who received it.

But it is replied, 'If reason be adequate, where is the necessity for revealed doctrines?' Might it not as well be asked, If reason be adequate, where is the necessity for the discoveries of scientific men? The 'adequacy of reason,' if we must adopt the phrase, does not mean that the reason of every child of man is adequate to discover all the mathematical and scientific and ethical truths which the world possesses. To one great man is given the power of making some great discovery or revelation. That discovery is tested by others, and acknowledged by the most capable men to be true. It enters the schools, and descends into the community. It is taught authoritatively in primers and lesson-books, and is received and professed by all. 'Revelation has a constant tendency to become nature—that is, to transmute itself, as it were, into our human flesh and blood and become part of our ordinary intelligence.'[1] In other words, revealed religion becomes natural religion. But the great majority of mankind could not have discovered it for themselves; and, although it can be verified by the reason, the great majority could not even verify it

[1] Christlieb.

except by experience. By the adequacy of the reason, we mean that the great truths which have been discovered and revealed by great men or inspired men— at least discovered and revealed in accordance with the mind and law of God—may be verified by the right use of a reason powerful enough to handle intelligently subjects of such a nature.

The one ever-speaking revelation of the mind of God is the history of man. It is the history of Divine rewards and punishments. In the growth and decay of nations, in the developments of conscience, in the achievements of art, in the happiness or discords of society, in the discoveries of science, in the efforts, successes, and failures of religions, we have the providential manifestation of the mind of God, the great Bible, of which our Bible is the most precious part. And for these unveilings of the Divine will and law let us be grateful. 'If we miss the truth,' says Jeremy Taylor, 'it is because we will not find it; for certain it is that all that truth which God hath made necessary he hath also made legible and plain, and if we will open our eyes we shall see the sun, and if we will walk in the light we shall rejoice in the light.' The way of salvation is a clearly marked way. It is not a series of mysteries which we cannot comprehend but must assert on pain of perdition.

Believe it not:
The primal duties shine aloft—like stars;
The charities that soothe, and heal, and bless,
Are scattered at the feet of man—like flowers.

> The generous inclination, the just rule,
> Kind wishes, and good actions, and pure thoughts.
> No mystery is here.

Mystery there must be, but thank God for revelation which has come ' to give light to them that sit in darkness and in the shadow of death, and to guide our feet into the way of peace.'

IV.

LIBERALISM IN RELIGION.

I.

'Handle me and see.'—*Luke* xxiv. 39.

WHETHER it is to be regretted or not, it is undeniable that members of the Church of England are not all of the same mind on certain religious subjects; just as it is certain that there never was a Church or sect in which different schools and parties did not exist. In our own Church these differences are seen from without as three great groups. Not that there are really sharp lines dividing them, for they intermingle with and gradually shade off into each other; but roughly they may be regarded as compact parties which have names by which they are known, as Gallican and Ultramontane denote or denoted bodies of opposing thought in the Roman Church. The names which have been given to the three great parties in our own Church may not be the most appropriate, just as the names Liberal and Tory may of themselves very inaccurately describe the great oppositions of modern politics. But it is hard to change these political terms and impossible not to use them. And exactly so is it with the names of our Church parties. Whether we like the names or not, we cannot help using them. It is of no use saying, when people wish to know what are our methods or conclusions in certain matters, 'We are Churchmen or Christians.' We cannot make ourselves understood unless we either use the distinctive name which will convey some of the information desired, or enter into long explanations of our private opinions—which, if they cannot be classed under any party, are probably but the vagaries of egotism.

Nobody disliked these names for Church parties more than Mr. Maurice, and no one was more unwilling to adopt such names. He utterly declined to be described as a Broad Churchman or one of the Liberal party. But it cannot be denied that he came to conclusions and interpretations, on religious and theological subjects, which were not those generally accepted by members of the Church of England, nor by the Protestant Dissenters of his time. It is certain he was a personage clearly marked off from the mass of religious teachers. He was much more clearly marked off, distinct, and original than Dr. Pusey was. No one can deny that his teachings on the word Eternal were not those generally received. We know that he suffered persecution because of these opinions. Dr. Jelf described them as 'very dangerous and unsound.' The Council of King's College pronounced them to be of 'dangerous tendency and calculated to unsettle the minds of theological students of King's College.' No one can deny that his teachings on the Atonement, which are now so widely diffused among all denominations of Christians, were shared in his day by but a few; they were condemned, as he painfully experienced, by many. 'Have you heard that Dr. Candlish came up to lecture against me at Exeter Hall ? . . . He was much applauded.'[1] Mr. Maurice was a profound philosopher and a profound theologian, and a man who lived in close and constant communion with God. In the devout use of his great powers he reached the conclusions which, he maintained, were the true teachings of Christianity, but which were not the conclusions of the great majority of Christians in any Church whatever. And in his letters he sadly admits his isolation. Here are the first words I light on to this effect. They are on Subscription, and he says, 'I had a moderately clear instinct when I wrote it that I never could be acceptable to any schools in the Church. . . . All these parties contain men at whose feet I am not worthy to sit. I have longed for sympathy with them all. But God has ordered it otherwise.' Well, it is indeed hard to give such a man a name, and that he lived a life above a name is evident in that he has left no school. His teaching and his spirit have entered into all schools and all parties, enlightening and sweetening all. 'The power of genius in history,' says Pfleiderer, 'is just this,

[1] Maurice, *Life*.

that it compels its very enemies against their will to submit to, to learn from, and to serve it.' But, as I have said, the conclusions Mr. Maurice reached, which to the majority seemed so original and to many so heretical, were reached by the devout and searching investigation of the Divine Oracles and of the history and products of the Church. He never professed to have had them given him by miraculous inspiration. They were the Divine rewards of toilful research, of reverent investigation, and of sympathetic openness of mind.

Now there are those in the Church, who at least in this respect—that is, in respect of method—claim to be his disciples. They may be far inferior to him, alike in natural power and in wealth of learning and in undivided singleness of aim. They may blunder, they may be rash and confident when they should hesitate, and they may speak when silence is a duty. But they do, with such learning as they possess, prayerfully turn them to the Divine revelations, in the Bible, in human history, and in the works of Nature, and seek to know the truth or to advance a step nearer to the truth. They do not believe that every accepted dogma of the past must, of necessity, be unmixed and infallible truth. It may be or it may not. But this they think is open to investigation and to verification. They do not believe that it is impossible to know more of God than was known in other days. They believe that there are new truths, and new aspects of old truths, which will be communicated to man, in accordance with God's method of educating the human race. They hold with Bishop Butler that it is not at all 'incredible that a book which has been so long in the possession of mankind should contain many truths as yet undiscovered. For all the same phenomena, and the same faculties of investigation, from which such great discoveries in natural knowledge have been made in the present and in the last age, were equally in the possession of mankind several thousand years before. And possibly it might be intended that events, as they come to pass, should open and ascertain the meaning of several parts of Scripture.' They do not look for a miraculous inspiration, but they do believe that reverent and capable investigation will be rewarded by Divine illumination. This, I say, was the method and spirit of Mr. Maurice, and it is the method and spirit of a party in the Church which is called sometimes the Broad Church party and sometimes the Liberal party.

Now the assailants of this party are never tired of declaring that its aim is to do away with Christian belief. A learned Roman Catholic writer, in a recent number of the 'Fortnightly Review,' declares that 'Liberal Protestantism obliterates the characteristics of the ancient creed,' and the same writer says that Protestantism would have been got rid of but for its Liberalism. 'Except for its Liberal tendency, the Reformed Churches could never have held out against the immemorial claims of Rome.' The one battle Cardinal Newman has been, he tells us, engaged in from Oxford days and the English Church to the Vatican and the Cardinal's hat, has been with Liberalism in religion. He says, 'I had fierce thoughts against the Liberals.' When he was indifferent to the teachings of the Fathers, and thought some of the verses of the Athanasian Creed 'too scientific,' he considered that he was 'drifting towards Liberalism in religion.' He asserts that the 'spirit of Liberalism is . . . the characteristic of the destined Antichrist.' He declared that, 'The vital question was, How were we to keep the Church from being Liberalised?' And he explains that, 'By Liberalism he meant the anti-dogmatic principle and its developments.' Even Mr. Maurice entertained some such idea of the Liberal party in his day, for he speaks of it as 'the party, which was emphatically anti-theological, which was ready to tolerate all opinions in theology only because people could know nothing about it.'

Now, if there were indeed in the Church a party opposed to dogma, a party opposed to theology, I myself should say that it was wrong that such a party should remain in the Church. But I do not think that there is such a party in the Church or ever has been. I maintain that Liberal Protestantism, Liberal Christianity, is not anti-dogmatic, is not anti-theological. There are anti-dogmatic teachers we know, anti-theological teachers we know. They mock at dogmas, and curl the lip of superfine scorn at theologies, but they have no place within the Church. They are not Liberals in religion. Their Liberalism, if it is Liberalism, is Liberalism without religion, it is irreligious Liberalism. Mr. Maurice really meant what are now called Agnostics when he spoke of the Liberal party as emphatically anti-theological, for he says it was so on the ground that 'people could know nothing about theology.' But the Liberalism within the Church does believe that it can know something about theology, gives its mind and soul to seek out more and more knowledge on such great subjects. It seeks for dogma; its prayer, its constant cry, is for a more revealing theology.

Now why is it that this party has aroused the suspicion in many minds that it is the enemy of Christian dogma, that it is anti-theological, that its principle is anti-dogmatic? It is, in a word, because it does not submit to every dogma and doctrine affirmed by the Churches, merely because those Churches affirm them. It maintains, with the Nineteenth Article of the Church of England, that 'as the Church of Jerusalem, Alexandria, and Antioch have erred; so also the Church of Rome hath erred, not only in their living and manner of Ceremonies, but also in matters of Faith.' It maintains, with the Twenty-first Article, that General Councils 'may err, and sometimes have erred, even in things pertaining unto God.' It cannot therefore believe in the infallibility of the Church of

England. But because Protestantism declines to submit to every Roman dogma, it is said to be anti-dogmatic. Because the Liberal Protestant declines, it may be, to accept certain dogmas affirmed by Luther or Calvin, or because he thinks that some dogmas or definitions or articles of religion might profitably be revised, so as more closely to represent the Divine Revelations, therefore he is called anti-dogmatic. He is said to be against all dogmas because, it may be, he denies some, just as the Prayer-Book denies 'the Romish doctrine concerning purgatory, pardons, worshipping and adoration, as well of images as of reliques, and also invocation of saints,' as 'repugnant to the Word of God;' or because he thinks that other doctrines might be drawn more accurately. But to call this spirit and temper anti-dogmatic is mere slovenliness of thought. To say it does away with the characteristics of the ancient creeds is childishness. It might as truly be said that the Prayer-Book is anti-dogmatic and does away with the characteristics of the ancient creeds. The characteristics of the ancient creeds are the positive facts they attempt to exhibit. Their authority is, as the Church positively teaches, that 'they may be proved by most certain warrants of Scripture.' But if some one endeavours to exhibit these facts still more clearly, who ought to say that his real aim is to obscure them or to destroy them? It might as well be said that the astronomers who proved that the sun is the centre of our system, were in fact secretly determined to get rid of the sun; that because they had renounced the ancient dogma that the earth is the centre of the system, they had renounced all astronomic dogma, and were anti-dogmatic; and that in a little time, when they had rubbed down the earth by their ceaseless attrition, and it had disappeared in the infinite, these astronomic Liberals —having respect for nothing decided—would soon turn their hands against the sun, and that 'they love darkness rather than light because their deeds are evil.'

Now I am positively for dogma, and so I am sure is every Liberal Christian, because a man cannot be a Christian at all without explicitly or implicitly holding Christian dogma. Every one must admit that there cannot be a Christian community without some Christian belief, some Christian intention. It is Christian because it has some faith in Christ, because it recognises some relationship to Him. If it says, 'Christ was the best and noblest man that ever lived, Christ is to be taken by all men as their example;' if statements like these, which we can imagine many Unitarians making, really state the grounds of some Christian union, they are dogmas. For what are dogmas? They are the formal statement of something which a society or class of men holds to be positively true. It is possible for men to *feel* that a thing is true, simply to apprehend it, without thinking about their own apprehension or putting it into words. This feeling is 'the shadow of those truths which unlearned piety admits and acts upon without the medium of intellectual representation.'[1] But the moment men unite in an expression of what they believe to be true, or rather of what they feel as truth and apprehend as truth, they give utterance to a dogma. A Unitarian is in principle no more anti-dogmatic than we Trinitarians. When you say, 'There is none other God but one,' or 'that God is Almighty,' or 'that He pardons iniquity, transgression, and sin,' or 'that the soul of man is immortal,' you are giving expression to what you hold to be truths. They are dogmas. If you teach these truths to other people your teaching is dogmatic teaching. There can be no other teaching. I subscribe without reservation to Cardinal Newman's declaration, 'Dogma has been the fundamental principle of my religion; I know no other religion; I cannot enter into the idea of any other sort of religion; religion, as a mere sentiment, is to me a dream and a mockery. As well can there be filial love without the fact of a father, as devotion without the fact of a Supreme Being.'

Dogmas are human attempts to express in words facts which the mind perceives. If you do see certain things, you cannot help expressing them. Your prayers, your teachings, all contain implicit dogma. If you cry 'Our Father,' your intellect will

[1] Newman.

affirm the proposition that God is the Father of all His creatures. And yet such words as dogma, orthodoxy, theology, excite a mocking smile in many a face which looks as though it had a mind behind it. Not every lawyer who sits in the House of Lords is omniscient, even if he 'look wiser than any man could possibly be.' And it is a melancholy sight, as it is an unusual one, to see a judge trying to amuse an assembly, whose manners he has scarcely yet acquired, by comparing theology to astrology. Professor Freeman says that 'law has ceased to be an empirical trade and become a science.' It can scarcely be so when a legal peer can openly gibe at the loftiest conceptions of the human mind. Paul and Athanasius and Augustine and Aquinas and Calvin were neither fools, nor verbal jugglers, nor manipulators of legal fictions, nor dupes. However they expressed themselves—and lawyers can scarcely be hard upon barbarities of style—they knew they were dealing with facts, with Eternal Verities; and so did their disciples; and so did the millions who might not be able to grasp their scientific expositions, but who did realise the truth itself. Only a man who can stand securely upon nothing, 'dance on the torrent and ride on the air,' can be independent of dogmas.

Here is another sample of unintelligent flippancy, 'Comfort benumbs the consciousness as orthodoxy benumbs the reason.' Now orthodoxy is that which, at any time, is held for true. It is a system of convictions received as true—evidently true to the scientific investigator, and accepted as true by the ordinary public. This is the state of things, for instance, with scientific conclusions or historical conclusions which are held to be correct. Would any rational man say that to hold correct conclusions in scientific matters 'benumbs the intellect,' or to have an accurate knowledge of history benumbs the intellect—in other words, that scientific or historical orthodoxy 'benumbs the intellect'? And why should it be any more true that theological orthodoxy benumbs the intellect? If any sort of orthodoxy forbids examination, re-investigation, then of course it benumbs the intellect; otherwise it might be said that to believe in gravitation benumbs the intellect. Speaking with less than his usual care, Dr. Martineau has given countenance to the objection to dogmas and creeds. He says the 'tendency to persecution exists wherever there is an incorporated clergy whose Church embodies a creed in its constitution.' Then every Church has a tendency to persecution—Dr. Martineau's as well as yours and mine—for there cannot be a Church which does not embody a creed. A Unitarian Church is neither Mussulman, nor Buddhist, nor Parsee, but Christian. In other words, it differs from these religions by some profession of Christianity. It has some Christian faith, a Christian creed, implicit if not explicit. It could not be a Christian Communion without some Christian standing ground or belief.

Even the late Principal Tulloch falls into a similar error, 'Unity can never come from dogma, as our forefathers unhappily imagined. Dogma splits rather than unites from its very nature. It is the creature of the intellect, and the intellect can never rest.' Can this be true? It may be true that the whole system of dogma imposed upon her children by the Roman Church, allowing of no inquiry, no re-examination, may provoke rebellion. But it is not true that dogma splits, that formal, accurate knowledge splits. Each new truth ascertained and made clear removes a cause of contention. It is the uncertain, the undecided, over which men wrangle and fight. But if such dogmas as these can be laid down as certain—yet open without hindrance to examination that all may prove them over again if they will—That there is one God who is the Father of all, and the Saviour of all, because the inspiring, ruling Spirit in all—if thousands and millions can see these truths and rest upon them, and, when it is necessary, can declare them as their undoubting faith, then these dogmas, instead of splitting, *unite*, and men become one in Christ Jesus. It is as true to say that such dogma splits as to say that identity of opinion divides men into opposite parties.

V.

LIBERALISM IN RELIGION.

II.

'Handle me and see.'—*Luke* xxiv. 39.

THERE are two grounds on which men assent to dogmas. One is that they are declared to be true by a competent authority. The other is that their truth commends and asserts itself to the human understanding. Rome declares herself a competent and sufficient authority. She demands faith in herself as a sufficient authority, and she requires that whatever she puts forth as truth shall be received and professed on her sole authority. And the reason she condemns Liberalism in religion as anti-dogmatic and destructive of the faith is, that Liberalism in religion does not recognise her authority, accepts no dogma whatever on the mere authority of a Church. It does recognise the truth of many Roman dogmas, but it does so, not because Rome says they are true, but because they can be shown to be true, because they take hold of the human understanding with convincing power. It is because they are true, and not merely because somebody says they are true, that Liberal Protestantism accepts them.

Now there is a suspicion in Roman minds that many of their dogmas cannot be shown to be true, that they may not commend themselves to the human understanding. They are afraid that if the spirit of Liberalism in religion turns its examining gaze upon them, they will be seen to be corruptions and not legitimate developments of Christianity. Therefore they cry out, 'This Liberalism is hostile to the faith.' But let not our High Church and our Low Church brethren stand apart from Liberalism as though they were not suspect. The charges which are made against Liberal Christianity are in fact, and indeed in word, made also against all Protestant Christianity; and Protestant Christianity is that Christianity which, as a consequence of the Reformation, is now separated from Rome. The Anglican who denies Transubstantiation is as much a Protestant in the eyes of Rome as the Evangelical who denies Baptismal Regeneration. With Rome every form of Christianity is Protestantism which, using its mind, ventures to deny anything which she has affirmed, and High Anglicans must bear the reproach of being Protestant as well as their Low Church brethren.

'The spirit of Liberalism is the characteristic of the destined Antichrist,' says Newman. 'Antichrist is described as the ἄνομος, as exalting himself above the yoke of religion and law. The spirit of lawlessness came in with the Reformation, and Liberalism is its offspring.' Again he says, 'I am more certain that the Protestant spirit leads to infidelity, than that which I recommend leads to Rome.' And again, 'I came to the conclusion that there was no medium, in true philosophy, between Atheism and Catholicity, and that a perfectly consistent mind, under those circumstances in which it finds itself here below, must embrace either the one or the other.' And another Roman Catholic writer says that 'the Reformation was anti-Christian in its nature, as all the world sees it to be in its results.'

There is one short answer to be made to the charge, that Protestantism leads to infidelity, and it is this. There is ten times more Christian belief in the countries which are Protestant than in the countries which are Catholic. If you want to see a generally diffused and largely operative Christian faith, you must go to the English-speaking races—in Great Britain, in the United States, in Australia and in New Zealand. This great people—one people, however various their forms of government—this mightiest race in the world, to whom the future belongs, has been fed on Protestantism, part of it on the very strongest and most uncompromising form of Protestantism. And this mighty, world-pervading, all-conquering race, the offspring of Protestantism, is far less influenced by unbelief than races like the Romance races, which have been formed by the discipline of Rome. When it is said that there are a less number of 'completely emancipated minds' in Protestant countries than in Roman Catholic countries, it means, that the number of infidels in Protestant countries is smaller than in Roman Catholic countries. Is there more Christian faith in France than in Scotland, or in Italy than in New England? It is idle to answer such questions. It is Rome which is the parent of infidelity, Rome which has made it malignant, and Protestantism which has saved the faith. It is high time that this talk of Protestantism leading to infidelity should cease. At least it is time for Rome to become silent in the presence of all the infidelity which has sprung up on ground which has been all her own.

But is there not something suspicious in the fact that Romanists and infidels alike are always telling us that we have no logical standing-ground, and that we ought to be either Romanists or unbelievers? Well, we are not going to be either the one or the other. And that which irritates them is that we *have* a standing-ground, that at least we manage to stand, and that we help others to stand also. 'If it were not for you,' cries the Romanist, ' millions would have been within the bosom of the Church who now are its foes.' 'If it were not for you,' cries the irritated unbeliever, 'thousands who could not have breathed in the stifling chambers of Rome would now have been free from all religious influences.'

I think we may thank God that such things can be said against us. Long may it be true that we do keep men from the sleepy lotus-land of Rome, and from the stony desert-land of materialistic infidelity. The Romanist has renounced his mind and envies our intellectual liberty. The infidel has lost his religion and envies the higher life of the emotions which we enjoy. We keep our mind and our soul; and the foes cry out, 'It is not fair, you have only a right to one of them.'

The reason Protestantism is charged with producing infidelity is that it claims the right of examining and reinvestigating, whenever it feels called to do so, whatever the Church may put forth as dogmas or certain truths. 'If you examine,' says Rome, 'you are certain not to believe.' But why? Is our faith a tissue of lies? Is there nothing in it which is sure and immovable? Can it not bear to be tested, and will searching investigation show it to be an imposture, words which are deceiving because they have no corresponding reality? It is a libel on Christianity to say any such thing, a libel which comes the worse from Christian lips. It is not Liberals in religion who say that free investigation will destroy Christianity, it is Romanists and unbelievers. On the contrary, we believe that the prime truths of Christianity are as positive and as verifiable as the ascertained truths of physical science. Science does not say, 'The law of gravitation is this, but for God's sake do not examine into the matter.

If you examine, you will not believe in gravitation, you will be destroying yourself, and jumping off a house or walking over a precipice.' 'Every halting-place in the course of rational inquiry,' says romantic infidelity in the person of M. Renan, 'is arbitrary.' You might as well say that when a man runs his head against a stone wall his stoppage is purely arbitrary. 'The truth once possessed,' says Professor Mozley, 'is seen to rest upon grounds of natural reason.' 'There is, perhaps, no greater satisfaction to the Christian mind than that which arises from perceiving that the revealed system is rooted deep in the natural course of things.'[1] 'It may be even questioned whether there be any essential character of Scripture doctrine which is without its place in this moral revelation.'[2] But if the truth be rooted in the 'natural course of things,' if it be seen to rest upon 'grounds of natural reason,' then it may be verified by appeal to the 'natural reason' and to the 'natural course of things.' We are surrounded by positive facts which produce religion, and the more we examine, the more certain are we to be confronted by these everlasting facts. Because we know we are dealing with eternal realities, we are not afraid that they will disappear if we look at them. Facts do not tremble for their existence. It is true that Rome fears inquiry, but Liberal Christianity does not.

[1] Newman. [2] *Ibid.*

'Private judgment,' says a Roman Catholic writer, 'is fatal to the notion of a society like the Catholic Church with its objective and infallible creed.' Again, the same writer says, 'Should the Roman Church fall, the Christian religion cannot as a religion live after it.' And Cardinal Newman naïvely confesses in the 'Apologia' that he determined to be guided by his reason, and that, had it not been for this severe resolve, *he would sooner have become a Catholic.*

It is implied by Roman Catholic writers, when it is not explicitly asserted, that if it had not been for the Divine authority conferred on the Church, the doctrines of Christianity would have been destroyed. 'Creeds would have long since been extinct but for the Apostolic Succession of Rome.' In this case these creeds cannot have become necessary to the world, the world cannot have found in them the supply for its spiritual wants and the answers to its most urgent questions. These creeds cannot have justified themselves in the experience of mankind, or they could stand firm and indestructible on that foundation. They have, so we are told, to stand on the Apostolic Succession of Rome, or they would fall. But this Apostolic Succession is not a thing which can be verified and proved positive in individual experience. It must submit to critical investigation; and, on such a subject, one student will have one conclusion and another a different one. If the creeds stand on Apostolic Succession alone, they have no sure foothold.

Yes, we can understand the terrors of Rome when threatened by free inquiry and examination. It is true that, as far as some Roman dogmas are concerned, Protestantism may be called anti-dogmatic. The Church has dared to dogmatise on matters which have not been revealed. She has pushed through the veil of the Temple into the Holy of Holies, and dealt with the High and Lofty One that inhabiteth eternity as though He were a subject for the biologist. And there are Roman dogmas the truth of which all forms of Protestantism deny.

Remember the New Testament reveals truth but seldom in the shape of dogma. 'The Scriptures were never intended to teach doctrine, only to prove it.'[1] The doctrines or dogmas of the Churches are man's formal statements of, and conclusions from, Divine revelations. Now man may err. He may draw false conclusions from positive truths. He is very likely to do so when he only knows fragments of truths, and not the truth in its perfect unity. He may take that for a cause, or an active factor, which may be modified by some other factor of which he is ignorant. He cannot say always, 'Because this is, that must be,' for he does not know all that is contained in the *is*. Cardinal Newman says, 'The doctrines of theological science are true if rightly deduced, because they are deduced from what is true.' In this case their truth is made

[1] Newman.

to depend on a correct process of reasoning. But this is Liberalism in religion. We say that some of the dogmas of Rome are not true—as, for instance, the doctrine of Transubstantiation—because they are not 'rightly deduced from what is true.' And, again, there are other dogmas which contain truths, but which are so expressed as to be misleading, or to conceal the truth they should clearly manifest. These dogmas in some cases want re-expressing, so that men may see that they are real truths. There are cases in which the Church has had glimpses of great truths, but she has generalised too soon, she has made a formula before she possessed sufficient material for a judgment. It has been the same in physical science. Great truths were pointed at in the Ptolemaic system of astronomy, but the system was a premature and incorrect generalisation. So, too, has it been with diverse Christian doctrines. Here are two authorities, both unimpeachable. The first, Dr. Ward, in a book so Romanistic in its teaching as to result in its condemnation by the University of Oxford, and in which none need fear a taint of Liberalism, says, 'The doctrine which supports men's spiritual life, the principle on which they live, may very easily be true, while the language in which they have learned to clothe it may be almost to any extent erroneous and dangerous.' And Dr. Swainson, in his most valuable book on the Creeds, asks, 'May it not become necessary in formulæ handed down to us to correct a shadow here, to erase a line there, to bring out a feature more prominently in another place, even as Augustine corrected Athanasius, and the aged Augustine corrected the young Augustine's writings?'

The supreme aim of Liberalism in religion is to get more certain hold of positive truth, and that will be the foundation of dogmas which can fear no examination. It may be that some of the doctrinal formulæ of the past may be shown to be erroneous conclusions from revelation, and others but imperfect representations of revelation. But the end will be, that if fewer things may positively be affirmed, and some things which have been looked upon as dogmas take the place of pious opinions, or of 'speculative expansions,' the firm foundation will be seen to be secure, and on that foundation union will be possible. The method of authority has been tried and failed. We must try the method of science, the method of unfettered examination. It tends to unity in physical researches, and if that which religious men seek to understand is positive, is real—real as the entities from which we obtain the laws of science—then faith in God will be seen to have no less sure a foundation than faith in the Cosmos; the mode of God's manifestation in history, I mean the revelation of the Trinity, will be more certain than the laws of physical development; and the salvation of Christ as sure in its action as the movements of the heavenly bodies. Authority has resulted in dead submission or in open rebellion. Free and capable investigation will result in a unity which cannot be broken.

But it is said, 'Liberals reject the idea of mystery.' Far from it. Spreading around the truths which have been revealed, which we can affirm and which are dogmas—indeed, concerning which disagreement is impossible—there is a land which grows less clear, then clouded over and dark. But we are certain that there is firm land there also. We believe that the day will come when it will be taken possession of, and that which is now obscure will be radiant with light. And yet we know that, when we occupy the land which to-day is enveloped in mystery, a new land of shadow and darkness will still girdle us round, and beckon us on to ever-renewed investigation. 'Canst thou by searching find out God?' 'Canst thou find out the Almighty to perfection? Clouds and darkness are round about Him, righteousness and judgment are the habitation of His throne.'

I.

DOES IT MATTER WHAT A MAN BELIEVES?

'With the heart man believeth unto righteousness.'—*Romans* x. 10.

IN what violent opposition to the spirit of the present day are the 'damnatory clauses' of the Athanasian Creed! How fierce and intolerant and false they sound in the ears of a languid superficial generation, which is too sensitive and too enlightened for any other creed than this—that it really does not very much matter what a man believes! I will admit that these 'damnatory clauses' were the product of Provincial rudeness; that to the unknown author of them they represented a quality of meaning we, happily, realise but imperfectly; that to ordinary hearers they impart unnecessary and improper alarm, and thus these clauses may render this creed unedifying in common worship—all this I am ready to allow. But I do say these same clauses, however objectionable their form, contain and proclaim a truth on which all creeds and systems of social well-being, good or bad, true or untrue, take their stand—that what we believe becomes the texture of our mind and the law of our conduct—in a word, settles our state; that a wrong belief, a mistaken belief, must put us upon a wrong tack, lead us to a wrong place, and that, *as long* as we have a wrong belief, our state and position must be wrong. I am amazed to find myself the apologist of phrases which I have always trembled to use, and which are an offence by which many a brother has stumbled. As they are commonly understood, they convey ideas which now revolt the sensitive Christian mind, and force it to say, 'They cannot be true.'

And yet there is truth in them. If I may say so, the nucleus of them is a truth. That nucleus may be held in a barbaric form. It may be that the form was that of which the unknown author only or mainly thought. But if ever the essential truth disguised by these clauses needed asserting, it is in days like these of stripling infidelity, when universal knowledge can be had from a newspaper and any man can be sceptical for a shilling. The more I think of it, the more I see that these clauses deal with conduct and the influence of belief upon conduct. For they speak about being 'saved,' they say that if certain things are not believed faithfully a man 'cannot be saved.' In other words, they speak of certain moral and spiritual states, and they say those moral and spiritual states can only be gained in a certain way. Just as we say, it is impossible for a man to be a great scholar without work, impossible to be saved from ignorance without using the proper means; so these formidable phrases declare that a certain moral and spiritual state, which is described as being saved, can only be reached in a certain way, and that as long as a man does not take that way he cannot reach that destination. Why, in essence, it is only what is declared by every reformer, revealer, and moral teacher. They all say, unless you adopt my scheme, my plan of life, of society, you cannot be all you might be; you must fail of the peace and perfection of your life —in other words, you cannot be saved. Here is the Athanasian anathema which Schopenhauer appends to his Teutonic Buddhism. 'Thus the *only way of salvation* is that the will shall manifest itself unrestrictedly,' &c. Mark, 'the only way of salvation.' Mr. Herbert Spencer teaches that we can only be saved from absurdity by a particular belief. 'Not he who believes that adaptation will increase is absurd, but he who doubts that it will increase is absurd.' 'The truths of science will save you,' declares a recent writer on the 'Creed of Science.' 'They will save your soul in the only way it can be saved.' Mr. Froude says that 'Carlyle's faith . . . was that, without a spiritual belief, a belief in a Divine Being, in the knowledge of whom and in obedience to whom mortal welfare alone consisted, the human race must degenerate into brutes.' Radically, the very same thing is asserted alike by Positivist and by Catholic. The damnatory clause is in essence—rude and misleading as is its form of expression—a statement of the law of cause and effect in morals, it is a special instance of the uniformity of Nature. Slipshod indolence and short-sighted frivolity may be unable to perceive the necessary connection between cause and effect in ethics; they may say it does not matter what a man believes; but science and practical wisdom, with or without faith in God, cannot say so. They must believe that there are such things as *necessary* truths, truths necessary, that is, for certain purposes, and that without certain beliefs a man cannot be saved.

For belief is inseparably connected with conduct; belief is the potentiality of action. With certain beliefs certain actions are quite impossible, they could not take place. Here are two authorities on this subject, neither of whom can be suspected of theological proclivities. 'No belief is real unless it guide our actions.'[1] 'Preparedness to act upon what we affirm is admitted on all hands to be the sole, the genuine, the unmistakable criterion of belief.'[2] All this is plain in everyday life. If you believed that the building in which you are seated was mined, and would be blown up in a few minutes, that already the fuse was lighted to fire the charge, what instant activity to escape would arise! If you were a large shareholder or depositor in a bank, and were told by the directors, who knew all the secrets of its management, that it was really insolvent, and believed what you were told; if you believed that the child of your love was hanging

[1] Professor Bain.   [2] Professor Clifford.

from a window-ledge ready to drop,—would your conduct be altogether uninfluenced by your belief? You believe that some one is bent on your ruin, and that another is a true friend who uses every opportunity to push your fortune and honour your name. You believe that such a one is a liar and a thief, and that this man has a lofty soul. You believe that certain measures are in the direction of social well-being and are demanded alike by generosity and justice, or, on the contrary, that they are the ignoble tribute paid to disloyalty. Is it not certain that your conduct will show marks of these various beliefs? Is it possible that you would feel and act in precisely the same way if you did not believe these things or believed the opposite? Would it make no difference whether you believed the glass which is held to your lips contained poison or precious medicine? Whether your beliefs are right beliefs or not—I mean whether they are in accordance with facts or not—if they are real beliefs, you are altogether made by them, your conduct is decided by them. They may be madman's beliefs, but they make the madman's life. By your beliefs, your happiness and nobleness, or your misery and degradation are decided. It may be that one single wrong belief has led you astray, given the wrong turn to your life, which has ever wandered farther from the right path, and has entangled you in labyrinths and thickets which bewilder you and make you despair. It may be a single belief which once held you, which now you see has kept you from success, placed you in a position you hate, dragged you down and ruined you.

Even accidental misbeliefs may bring condign punishment. A train stops in the night on a viaduct, and the coping of the bridge is taken for the platform of the station, and the lamps are too distant to show the black abyss, and one confidently steps out, and into quick destruction. A mistaken belief may make a very hell on earth, and in such a case as that of Othello 'doth work like madness in the brain.' In the affairs of this life, whether you believe in God or not, you must have a right creed or suffer, a right creed or perish. If there is no life after this, and if this life—the only life—be spoilt by a wrong belief, then in this case a wrong belief, a mistaken belief, has wrought irrecoverable ruin. Stern Nature thunders forth her damnatory clauses. She tortures and kills and buries out of sight those whose actions proceed on a false belief. It is as true of nations as of individuals. Look at their faiths, and you will see the arbiters of their destiny. The real belief of a people is that which is moving it on to greatness or decay. 'It has not been a mistake or a delusion,' says Mr. Maurice, 'into which men have fallen, when they have traced all the moral evils of the world, all its political evils, to its superstitions; that is to say, to its false notions of God;' and Mr. Froude affirms that 'Illustrious natures do not form themselves upon narrow and cruel theories.'

> Oh purblind race of miserable men,
> How many among us at this very hour
> Do forge a life-long trouble for ourselves
> By taking true for false, or false for true ![1]

If there is a false saying, as far as this human life is concerned, it is that 'It does not matter what a man believes.'

But not only do misbeliefs produce misconduct, but there is also to be taken into account the deteriorating influence they have upon the mind itself. Each new belief which takes possession of the mind tends to rearrange its parts or to modify their colour and their quantity. Bear in mind that I am speaking of those comparatively few intense realisations which alone properly deserve to be called belief. Many of us are indeed nothing but

> Light half-believers of our casual creeds,
> Who never deeply felt, nor clearly will'd;
> Whose insight never has borne fruit in deeds,
> Whose vague resolves never have been fulfill'd.[2]

I cannot now stop to maintain, what here I shall only affirm, that belief is certitude. Belief is not a mode of probability, it is a complete supreme act which fills the mind and moves it to confident action. Belief is the grasp of the whole nature, of head and heart combined; it is certitude, well put in the words of St. Paul, 'I *know* in whom I have *believed.*' These few beliefs, these energising realisations, infect the whole mind; they act upon neighbouring parts, they add a new

[1] Lord Tennyson. [2] Mr. M. Arnold.

element to all which was there before, they have their own affinities, drawing after them that with which they naturally combine, until the whole being is correlated to the new belief. Now that a new belief has entered, modifying and rearranging the mental structure, it must be taken into account in every emergency, it goes along into the world of action with all the other beliefs which it allows to live. The loss of a belief may be a good thing or a bad thing, it cannot be an indifferent thing. A new belief makes a new creature. Mr. Lecky says, 'He can have observed human nature with but little fruit who has not remarked how very rarely men change fundamentally the principles they had deliberately adopted on religious, moral, or even political questions, without the change being preceded, accompanied, or very speedily followed, by a serious modification of character.'

It is a strange thing how beliefs hang together, and are found in cliques. I suppose it is the result of unconscious logic. Follies, like sheep, are gregarious. When you know that some man advocates an evident quackery, you may be certain that he carries appeals for ever so many more in his pocket. A tenderness for small-pox will extend its sympathy in kindred directions, and Millenarianism probably be combined with strong opinions on the 'Ten Tribes' and a deep interest in 'Psychical phenomena' and in Esoteric Buddhism. 'Unsound opinions,' said Sir George Lewis, 'have a certain affinity with one another, and are formed in knots and clusters.' They draw after them falsehoods with which they have affinities, they gradually pervert the whole nature; and when an evil spirit is allowed admittance, he holds back the door until his accomplices have got within. So much does it matter, as far as our mental and moral constitution are concerned, what a man believes.

If, then, our belief decides our conduct, and converts and reconstructs our character, it must be evident, even to the most sceptical, that our religious beliefs must be potent factors in shaping our destiny. Only the flippancy of fools can say that it does not matter what a man believes in religion. But a deeper and more reverent spirit may peradventure be moved to ask, Are there indeed, as orthodox teachers have so strongly maintained in the past, '*necessary* doctrines,' as well as *unessential* doctrines, and is the doctrine of the Trinity a necessary doctrine? Now if by 'necessary doctrine' be meant *true* doctrine, then every doctrine, which reveals itself to a man as truth, is a necessary doctrine. The moment a thing is seen to be true it is as necessary as any other truth. In this sense the smallest truth which the mind perceives as truth is necessary to salvation—that is, to salvation from some ignorance, and to salvation from untruthfulness of spirit. To turn away from a truth which commends itself to our acceptance is immoral, and so long as a man consciously turns away from a truth he is unsaved, he is a criminal infidel. Whether we like the truth or not, whether or not it fits in with our previous opinions or plans of life, our prospects of preferment or promises of peace and pleasure, if we turn aside our face from a truth which meets us and for a moment looks into our eyes, then, however apparently unimportant that truth, it is most important for us; and if we reject it, we condemn ourselves as unfaithful.

When we are told that a doctrine or truth is necessary, a question properly suggests itself, 'Necessary for what?' For one doctrine is necessary for one thing and another for another. That we should hold truth as to the constitution of things, especially those which form our practical environment, we have already seen to be necessary. But if the constitution of things is but one aspect of the mind and will of God, if the great fact of the universe, the embracing, constraining, never-absent fact of the universe, fashioning us behind and before and laying its hand upon us, is God, then above all things, because including all things—alike actualities and potentialities—is it necessary that we should have true beliefs about God. If the doctrine of the Trinity is a revelation of that which is, and which was, and which is to come, then the doctrine of the Trinity is a necessary doctrine, necessary to bring us salvation from the fears and bondage which otherwise might overwhelm us; and to fight against it, must be to fight against the very nature of things. That doctrine through all its subtle explanations — explanations which are but human reflections of the Divine fact—declares to us the one Eternal Spirit and Eternal Law, in itself for ever inaccessible, the God who is called by some the Unknowable. It reveals to us God in man, intelligible and adorable and redeeming. And it reveals the reconciling and sanctifying Spirit proceeding from the Father and the Son—the Almighty Spirit which shall subdue all things unto itself that God may be all in all. If this be true, it is indeed a message of salvation. Not to know this, is to be without this message of salvation, and he who will not accept it must lose the blessing it can convey.

The doctrine of God's pardoning love to all mankind, which is the very essence of the doctrine of the Trinity—'for even Fathers and Schoolmen,' as Mr. Maurice reminds us, 'speak continually of the Trinity as the Eternal Charity'—is absolutely necessary to bring peace and assurance to a mind burdened with a sense of sin. If the sinner does not believe that there is a God who will wash away his sin, if he believes that by Divine sovereignty he is condemned to endless perdition, if he will not accept the true faith of the Trinity—of the Eternal Charity—that God loves and pardons His guilty children, then he cannot be saved from his despair, he will not take the salvation. If he will not believe that Christ hath redeemed all mankind, and that all his brethren are in the hands of the sanctifying Spirit, he must turn pessimist and despair for the race.

But the question, Does it matter what a man believes? usually implies in the mind of the speaker, Does it matter, as far as another life is concerned, what a man believes? Will men be sent to hell, as men once were condemned to an *auto da fé*, because they are misbelievers? Must heathens and Deists and Christian Unitarians and all who have imperfect or incorrect beliefs about God be sentenced to remain for ever in their ignorance, and to suffer for ever from its consequences? We know that mistaken beliefs, innocent or culpable, do bring punishment. If a man can take his mistaken beliefs into another world and retain them when there, as far as we can see, the same painful consequence which they produced here must ensue there. If, indeed, the doctrine of the Trinity reveals an eternal fact, then we must admit that, as long as men do not perceive this fact, do not believe it, and therefore do not act in accordance with it, they must be without the light and comfort and strength which this revelation is calculated to impart. They must suffer this loss so long as they do not accept that which alone can relieve them. For if the doctrine of the Trinity be a revelation of the Eternal, and if for everlasting ages a man were unable to accept it, then it would follow that for everlasting ages he must be without the special blessings which the truth alone can impart. The priests of Agnosticism are as threatening as those of Catholicism. One of them says, 'No real belief, however trifling and fragmentary it may seem, is ever truly insignificant; it prepares us to receive more of its like, confirms those which resembled it before, and weakens others; and so gradually it lays a stealthy train in our inmost thoughts, which may some day explode into overt action, and leave its stamp upon our character for ever.' But will men remain heathen, Deist, Unitarian, for everlasting ages, if these faiths are in conflict with eternal reality? Is the real never to conquer the unreal, and are errors for ever to maintain their existence in the full light of truth? There is a promise in the Bible which points to the ultimate triumph of truth in every human soul, for we are told that at the name of Jesus *every knee shall bow of things in heaven and things in earth and things under the earth, and that every tongue shall confess that Jesus Christ is Lord to the glory of God the Father.*

But the temper of mind represented by the question, Does it matter what a man believes? is an ignoble and base-born temper. In such a temper there is no principle and the way to dishonour is easy. 'The inquiry of truth,' says Bacon, 'which is the love-making or wooing of it; the knowledge of truth, which is the presence of it; and the *belief* of truth, which is the enjoying of it—is the sovereign good of human nature.' But he who thinks it does not matter what a man believes does not care about truth, is incapable of high feeling, of watchful rectitude, and of undefiled sincerity. Such a man is destitute of the 'sovereign good of human nature,' and until this corrupting temper is taken away the soul must be condemned to an ignoble life. But an ignoble life is not the life eternal.

VII.

COMMONPLACE BELIEF IN GOD.

I.

'And though they say, The Lord liveth; surely they swear falsely.'—*Jeremiah* v. 2.

I MAINTAINED in my last sermon that a man's belief affects his conduct, that ignoble beliefs tend to make ignoble lives; that untrue beliefs—that is, beliefs which are in opposition to the nature of things—pervert and may destroy a life; and that faith in such a revelation as that of Christianity, faith in the Trinity—Father, Son, and Holy Ghost, one God, blessed for evermore—saves a man from the terrors of superstition, from the bonds of evil, and from the impotence of despair. But I think it may be said by some, 'Are there not those who do not believe these doctrines, and who do not accept Christianity as a Divine revelation—that is, as revealing the foundation and constitution of things—who may call themselves Agnostics or be positively anti-Christian, who are quite as noble and self-sacrificing as the very best Christian that ever was? Are not the priests of Positivism as good men as those of

Catholicism, and the professors of Agnosticism as moral as the preachers of Protestantism?' Yes, thank God, it is so. Am I here to deny that goodness is goodness because it is allied to a faith which I do not share? Goodness, wherever it is found, is of God, whether men know it or not, and I bow to the manifestation of God's Holy Spirit, whether it be seen in Christian or unbeliever.

Indeed the non-Christian and anti-Christian teachers of the present day are after all the children of faith. Mostly born of Christian parents, and educated in Christian churches, and shaped by a literature whose roots have been planted in Christianity for a thousand years, and influenced by institutions and customs and modes of speech and manner, by, as I may say, an atmosphere which they have breathed ever since they were born—and for myself I must add, having within their very mental and spiritual structure the deposits of many generations, deposits from the ages of faith—such men can scarcely help being still to a very large extent Christian. They can no more help being Christian than an Englishman can help being an Englishman, even when he renounces his country and changes his dress and speaks with self-satisfied fluency an alien tongue. Nations and men are the products of many generations. They are a series of strata, one imposed upon the other. The unbelievers of the present day have taken off one stratum of their inherited character, but there are ever so many more below.

As our characters, yours and mine, are this very instant affected by twelve centuries of Christian influence, so it would take centuries to undo the work of Christ so as, at last, to leave our characters without one trace of His power. And do you think that the infidel scratchings and scrapings of one generation alone will do it? The noble ideals which fill the minds of those who in this day ignore or oppose Christianity have been made for them by Christianity, and we may honour the work of Christ and see the presence of His spirit in those who think they are independent of Him.

But, it may be said, the majority of those who are orthodox and attend churches and preach in pulpits do not differ from the ordinary run of those who are not orthodox and who do not attend churches. It may be said by some one, 'I know people quite well who believe all the articles of the Christian faith, and reprobate every heresy, who are not particularly pleasant or safe people to deal with. They are self-opinionated and ill-tempered. They are selfish, envious, overbearing. They are not loving and considerate and forgiving at home. They are eager to pamper and gratify themselves, requiring that all should give up for them and make way for them, but giving no help to make others happy. Their care for their own interest makes them keen and sly and underhand. They take unfair advantage and are untrue. They come to church, and patronise Bible Societies and missionaries, and have family prayers. But they are as heartless and haughty, as selfish and insincere, as prudently sensual and practically indevout, as the commonest clay, that finds a Sunday dinner more congenial than Sunday worship and has not said a prayer for years. Is it not clear that religious belief is really uninfluential? Take your own congregation, and take as many hundreds who sit in Club windows on Sundays, or who lounge at home over the "Field," or who in the country take a walk or look at the hounds while the ladies are at church—is it a fact that your congregation, at home, in Parliament, in professional or mercantile life, is something very different, very much finer and nobler, than those who know no worship? And if they are not, is not belief really without effect?'

Now in return let me ask such an one this question. Do you really think that if the majority of men believed in their very hearts, so, as it were, to see it day by day before them, that God Almighty was looking at them, standing by them, that they were responsible to Him, that they would give account to Him, that every sin they committed He would sooner or later punish, and that they could not evade that punishment as though God might forget or die—do you think that such a belief would make no difference to them? Let them believe, so as to be sure of it as of a friend's or mother's love, that that God, so near and so inexorably righteous, is also their Saviour, ready to help them to a finer, happier life; close to them each moment, speaking to them from His cross of a higher life, and a life for ever in heaven when death has blanched their cheeks and stilled their tongues—and would this make no difference? Let them believe, that that feeling towards something better is the very stirring within them of God's Holy Spirit, that in them now is the presence of God Himself bearing witness against the brute and the beast within them, contending with the devil in them which would sink them into loathsomeness and crime and damnation, and that in this world that Holy Spirit is ever working in accordance with Eternal Law for the perfection and happiness of man. Do you really think that all that, held before the mind as a fact, as clearly seen as the matter before your eyes, as inseparably present to the soul, so that in no place could men go, not even in the darkness where shamelessness seeks concealment, but that a man believed all that—God present, Christ beseeching, the Spirit making intercession with groanings which cannot be uttered—do you believe that all this would be nothing? Do you think that it would be just the same if a man believed there was no God, that conduct is a mere matter of taste—one man preferring duplicity and drunkenness and sloth, another liking study and sympathy and such things—that there is no order, no life to come, and, except to society, which can punish, no responsibility and no judgment day? You know it is quite impossible. Why, many of the noblest of those who have been unable to believe the things which Christians believe have declared they should like to believe them, that they wish they could believe them, and that it would be an unspeakable comfort if only they could believe them.

But, if it is true that the majority of us who recite the Creeds and believe the Articles and condemn all false doctrine, are really just as common and just as animal as the ordinary run of those who care for none of these things—and Bishop Hall has well said, 'Lewdness of life and practice may stand with orthodoxy in some main points of religion'—then it follows, not that belief is ineffective, but that we have no real belief; that, whatever we think we have, it is not belief, at least not belief in those things of which I have been talking; and an angel may be standing over our heads in church when we recite our belief, and he may be saying the words which the prophet said in days gone by, 'Though they say, The Lord liveth; surely they swear falsely.' Is this a harsh saying, that a very large number of those who profess to believe, in fact do not believe, are the victims of self-deception, are indeed infidels without knowing it—infidels preaching and infidels responding 'All this I stedfastly believe'? Then I will soften down the harsh statement. I will not be so abrupt as the prophet who declared that those who said the Lord liveth were perjurers. I will not say with Coleridge that we are 'orthodox liars for God.' Instead of the ancient prophet, I will take a phrase from a modern historian. Mr. Froude says of one of Queen Elizabeth's most trusted councillors, Sir Robert Cecil, that 'he believed in God in a commonplace way.' Instead of saying that many of us who profess Christian belief, in fact and in truth do not believe, I will say we believe in a commonplace way.

Let me describe this commonplace belief, or what Cardinal Newman has more accurately called 'notional assent.' It is the assent we give to something which is told us because we see no reason for thinking the thing untrue in itself, nor yet for calling in question the trustworthiness of the teller; we see no reason why we should deny it, it would imply more interest in the subject than we possess to deny it. We assent to it and forget all about it the next minute; we have other things to think about, other things to take into consideration, to arrange for, to be anxious about; but it makes no difference to us whether it is true or false. If we had been told the opposite we should have believed that in the same way, but it creates little or no interest in us one way or another. It neither excites our intellects nor warms our hearts. Yes, we believe what we have been told—that is, we do not disbelieve it—but if it is not true, things will go on much the same, however the question is decided. If I am told that 'magnetism is associated with electricity by its mechanical analogies, and still more closely by its physical influence,' or that the spectroscope has made known what but a few years ago Comte declared to be for ever beyond the reach of human knowledge, or that the authorship of the 'Imitation of Christ' has been finally cleared up, I assent. If the opposite of these things had been told me by what I took for competent authority, I should equally have assented. Just so with the religious truths which very early were impressed upon us. We do not doubt them, we do not often think of them, we do not want them disturbed, and we do not want them to disturb us. Such beliefs are not retained long before the mind, they do not become the centre of an intellectual interest, they do not regulate the conduct, they supply no place which without them would be left vacant. That is believing in a commonplace way. But let a man believe that the dearest being in all the world is unfaithful to him, and mocks at his fondness when he is absent, and boasts how easily he is duped. Let a beleaguered garrison closed in by ferocious enemies, with food and ammunition spent, at last about to give in and take its grim chance, unable longer to resist—let it for a moment believe that to-morrow help will come, let but the sounds of familiar notes be carried on the breeze to ears growing indifferent and dead, and men will start up and cry, and look strong, wasted and gaunt though be their frames, and beat the drums and shout defiance, till the waiting wolves around them, just ready to spring, are daunted. These are not commonplace beliefs; they are what I will call realistic beliefs.

Now I maintain that many of us believe in God in a commonplace way, and because we do so the sensualists around us, who only care to eat and amuse themselves, are right when they say that our belief makes us no better than they are. For, alas! it is true, men do not think upon God even as they think of their friends who are away, of their children and homes, or of the change of residence, or of the new start in life, or of the approaching loss of place, or of those they love now hidden in the grave. These things, one after another, float through their minds as they go to their business, or practise their art, or charm in society, but God they utterly forget. They do not do certain things, lest they should thereby displease an influential friend, or lose respect among their acquaintances; and some things they do, but they do them secretly lest their neighbours or constituents or customers or inferiors or children should know. But God is not worth considering. 'Tush, say they' in their hearts, in their forgetful practice, 'how should God perceive it, Is there knowledge in the Most High?' Oh yes, they believe in God, all powerful, all seeing, all judging; but they do not blush when they cheat or injure their fellows, or soil their bodies and souls in secret, *for no one but God will find it out.* It is quite possible that to many of us it would matter little if there were no God. We should be neither much better nor much worse. We should do the same work, think about the same things. We should only have to give up our private and family prayers, and perhaps that might almost be a relief. But there cannot be any worth in such a belief. If you do not believe in God as much as you believe in your children, your office, or your horse, how can you think that saying you believe in Him is a virtue which will secure your everlasting salvation?

> First amend, my son,
> Thy faulty nomenclature; call belief
> Belief indeed, nor grace with such a name
> The easy acquiescence of mankind
> In matters nowise worth dispute.[1]

We Protestants are in the habit of thinking that Roman Catholics, for the most part, are content with simply assenting to what the Church declares; with reciting forms of words, according to order, which are supposed to act like charms. We think that what the Church condemns is an unsubmissive spirit, and that she promises to secure the salvation of those who without question assent to her declarations. In other words, we think she teaches that the Church makes men free, and that Protestants, on the other hand, teach, with Christ, that it is the truth which shall make men free. May we not in this respect be unjust to the Roman Church, and may it not be true of ourselves that we trust in magic recitations? Take these

[1] Mr. Browning.

words of a doctor of the Roman Church. Speaking of one of the mysteries of the faith, he says, 'As well might this awful truth be disbelieved altogether as believed only by the head,' and that 'a practical realisation of it is the object to be desired.'[1] But, if this is so, this Catholic philosopher distinctly affirms, what I have been maintaining, that there is no virtue or value in a faith, even if it be true and of the most solemn importance, unless it is realised so as to rule the life. This Catholic says a man might as well disbelieve as believe without a practical realisation. And I say so too. In other words, a man may as well profess the Catechism of Comte as the Athanasian Creed or any other Christian creed, if the creed is ineffective.

And one thing more I will say in conclusion. It is quite possible for an unbeliever in Christianity to be more a Christian than some who profess Christianity. Our subject is commonplace belief. But there may be commonplace unbelief. An unbeliever may have a latent, but operative and real, Christian faith, and his unbelief may in fact be commonplace. It may be that the system of doctrine or philosophy professed by the unbeliever may be held by him in a commonplace way. He may teach that God is unknowable, and that morality in the long run is expediency, but all this may be on the surface and have no influence on his life. He may really feel the

[1] Dr. Ward.

wonder and bounty of Nature, and awe towards that which is behind Nature. He may recognise the ever-acting forces which tend to greater happiness and more perfect life. He may be content to sacrifice himself that some good may be gained by the future, that when he is no more, he may live again in the lives which he has blessed, but which will know him not. Such a man has realised certain truths of the Christian creeds, albeit he misunderstands their form, and it is the truth and not the form which makes us free. And it may be, too, that while the explicit faith of some of us who are believers is commonplace—that is, our faith in God and Christ is commonplace, an inoperative Sunday profession—our real belief may be atheistic. For if we are ruled by an indolent scepticism or an unrelenting egotism or a self-indulgent sensuousness, it may be said of us, 'Whose God is their belly, whose glory is in their shame, who mind earthly things.'

VIII.

COMMONPLACE BELIEF IN GOD.

II.

' The prophets prophesy falsely, and the priests bear rule by their means; and my people love to have it so: and what will ye do in the end thereof? '—*Jeremiah* v. 31.

'What will ye do in the end thereof?' If, now, the preachers pray and preach, and the people are gathered together in the churches, but if, notwithstanding, their belief is as though it were a no-belief, without practical effect—so that if in their sleep it were to pass quite away it would make no difference, leaving behind no aching void—what must such a state of things lead to? What will it be in our children, and what in generations to come? Will commonplace belief in God have power to hold its own, or will the orthodox atheism of the present become the openly anti-Christian atheism of the future? What is the natural history of commonplace belief? I am persuaded that, of all the countries of Europe, at the present moment there is more real religion in Great Britain than in any other; that below this mass of realised belief there is a widespread, if commonplace and practically uninfluential, confession of Christianity; and that anti-Christianism is at present numerically small, is fairly courteous in its manners, and is yet without the malignity which in France, for instance, often shows itself as livid hatred of priests and Church and God—of what it calls Clericalism. How seldom do we see such scenes as those which are frequent in the great cemetery of Paris, when crowds are gathered together around the grave of philosopher, politician, or Socialist reformer, ostentatiously refusing the last ministrations of the Church, and with sentimental heroics rejecting the hopes of immortality. In what country of Europe possessing representative institutions will you see a duly elected member excluded for years from the Chamber because he is a dogmatic Atheist? I am expressing no opinion on the rights of the case. But I do say it is a tribute to the faith which remains or is thought to remain in the English race, for the fear of constituents in some cases has led members of Parliament, not overweighted themselves with dogmatic faith, to take the side of exclusion. You cannot imagine such a thing in Paris, in Rome, in Berlin.

It is true we have Anglicanism in England, Presbyterianism in Scotland, Romanism in Ireland, and Calvinistic Methodism in Wales. But in all there is a good deal of realised religion and a very general assent to a form of Christianity. Is there at the present moment a more orthodox or religious Roman Catholic country in the world than Ireland—a land which in centuries long gone by sent out her scholars and missionaries to every country in Europe, and was looked on by all as the land of saints? To the present day her children, high and low, are untinged with *heresy*, and are passionately devoted to their faith. We may attribute it to cruel persecutions in the past, to hatred of a conquering race and its religion, but there is the fact. Of the remaining Protestant parts of our common country, I am prepared to reaffirm that nowhere in Europe can you find so much real and so much honest conventional religion. The British Sunday is a perplexity no less than a purgatory to foreigners who have to endure it.

And yet how much we are divided, what numberless sects! What freedom of speculation is thus encouraged! In many churches, what an assimilation is there of the truths of science, and what an endeavour to lead the intellect of the nation! Where will you find so many men, eminent in science and art and the service of the State, who at the same time are humble Christians, as in Great Britain, her Colonies, and in the United States? These theological differences of ours are signs of faith. M. Renan has said, to ' innovate in theology is to believe in theology;' and these differences of ours, I venture to think, are but the necessary steps to unity in ascertained truth. That unity might possibly have been reached ere this, if the inquiries of the mind had not been gagged in days gone by, and its movements restricted until it had become numb and almost paralysed. Again to quote M. Renan, 'France is the country of all the world the most orthodox because she is the most indifferent in religion.' I suppose he means that those who profess any religious belief in France are the most orthodox; for, as the world knows, anti-Christianism of the most malignant kind is the very temper of the great cities. What he means is that those who conform to the Catholic Church, question nothing, accept whatever is said, and do not care enough to look into the matter or to disturb their minds. 'France is the most orthodox because she is the most indifferent in religion.' That is, her believers are believers in a commonplace way, and her unbelievers are the masses.

As a rule, intense, realistic faith is more likely to be found—special circumstances making special exceptions—and has a better chance in Protestant countries than in Catholic. Where belief means profession, or what Cardinal Newman calls 'notional assent,' and where this general assent with ritual conformity is generally regarded as sufficient, men are contented with themselves when they have done all that is required. And, having been brought up in the atmosphere of general assent, no need for apprehensive certainty, for embracing faith, is felt. True faith never exists, and yet there may be neither dissent nor heresy. But that passion to know, that love of truth, powerful as it is in Protestant countries, if it reduces the extent of faith, deepens the intent; that which is held is held tenaciously, not because it is a virtue to believe as many things as possible, but because truth is precious to the soul.

But my purpose is not to minister to that Pharisaic self-satisfaction which so often repels from Englishmen the sympathy of other nations; it is rather to sound a note of warning, by showing what must be the natural result of general commonplace belief. In the long run it must result in open, avowed infidelity. If, as a nation, we are now in the condition of reciting creeds and attending churches, but are untouched by them, uninfluenced in temper and taste and conduct by them, the natural results will be national infidelity and national apostasy. When I say the natural result I mean that, unless some Divine interposition take place, unless some outpouring and contagion of the Spirit of holiness work a revival of real religion, our present state of devout respectability and Sunday sanctity will gradually give place to offensive infidelity towards Christianity.

The path of descent which will be followed will have some such stages as these: First of all, carelessness in the matter of religious observance—now falling in with it, and now disregarding it. Already there are symptoms of this descent. It may be seen in the large neglect of that bond and symbol of Christian intention and brotherhood—the Sacrament of the

Eucharist. I know some are prevented from sharing in that Sacrament by perplexing uncertainty as to its meaning and obligation. But I think that the most careless of us would say that, except for such impediments, every very religious man, every man of real piety, whose belief in God and Christ lived in his soul like a fire, warming and kindling his whole nature, would delight in loving thanksgiving for the truth which had brought salvation. You would say, I know, whatever be your practice, that a man who really loved God, and was devoted to Christ, would find His Holy Communion a high and exalted privilege. But is it not a fact, too evident for speech, that tens of thousands of those who are quite orthodox, and dread these German writers, and these Ritualists and Freethinkers who 'ought to be turned out of the Church,' do pass by this ordinance of Christianity? They pass it by, and yet are perfectly certain that if they were very religious, if they really, realistically, believed in Christ, they would not pass it by.

It is said that in Catholic churches the women very vastly predominate in the congregations, and that the men are comparatively few. May not the same thing be said of our own churches in the matter of Holy Communion? And does not this fact point to the next development, that it will be the same in time with our own Sunday public worship as it is already with our more private Communion—that men will be rare? Even now, how many men there are who, when rebuked for neglect of Divine worship, reply, 'Oh, I always go to church when I am in the country or at the seaside.' In other words, there is nothing else to do, and you see everybody at church, and it gives you something to talk about, and it has not yet become quite the thing for ladies and gentlemen to fix their tennis 'tournaments' for Sunday mornings, using the church bell as the signal for assembling. 'And in the country we go to church; one ought to set a good example to one's tenants and the labourers, and back up the clergyman a little, who, after all, is a poor creature unless *we* stand by him—*lay assistance* is so very important, you know. But it is quite different in London. Nobody knows whether you go to church or not.' Here, you see, is no real faith in God, no devoted love of worship. Do away with such inducements as I have mentioned, and there would be as little church-going at the seaside and in the country as now in London.

And this temper, with its open inconsistency, tells upon children, who become still more indifferent than their parents. 'Why should they go to church, there can be no particular good in it? Their parents do not think there is much good in it, or else they would act differently.' Thus a generation must be produced altogether ignorant of Christianity or religion of any kind. When once you have reached the condition of things in which the men ignore worship of every kind and only the women frequent it, there gradually arises amongst the men secret dislike to religion, a dislike which now and again becomes audible. Really religious women become unhappy about their husbands and sons and brothers. Religion is something very solemn and very elevating and very saving, or it is a prodigal farce. In the latter case women too must fling it away. They will say, 'Why should women—mothers and maidens—be made fools of, and worship waxworks, and be fed on fables any more than men? Do men think that we need hoodwinking in order to keep us virtuous? Then they should be a little sharper if they intend to take in their weaker companions, and act as though they themselves believed.' If Christianity is all a fable and a fraud, why should not women speak of God and Christ as of any heathen god and Oriental wonder-worker? And if women are in the long run constrained to follow the indifference and unbelief of the men of their families, this will be the result. But if, on the other hand, they know in whom they have believed, and if they feel all the loss of ennobling influence, all the blindness to eternal fact and ever-acting Divine law which is perverting those who are dear to them, it will settle down upon them as pain and anxiety. It will make them warn and pray for those they love. There will be two opposite courses and dispositions in the home. There will be a separation in spirit which may never be spoken of, which may at length stir in the man irritation and anger and opposition to that which has produced the division. He will say, 'It is all these cursed priests with their wiles, leading captive silly women, and the world will never be happy until it is all got rid of. Voltaire said, If there were not a God we should have to make one; but we are far past that. We must get rid of such fragments of God as are left, for as long as relics remain, men will bow down to them, or rather women will. And so we must cleanse the schools from every contaminating remnant of God, and disendow the Churches, and make seminarists serve in the army, and in time we shall be rid of these bugbears which self-interested ecclesiastics have set up to serve themselves as well as civil despotisms.'

Can we see ourselves in these words? Do they sound like anarchism and nihilism? And yet to that will empty, unpractical profession of Christianity surely lead, and orthodox formality bring forth active and offensive atheism; and we conservative, conforming, mechanically devout members of the upper classes, who are too well off to need so much thinking as some people seem to require, indeed do not know why the classes below us need think at all, if only they are content with their lot and respect their betters—such may be the fathers or grandfathers of those to whom God will be a scoff, and immortality a fragment of old mythology, and judgment the bugbear which once was able to keep the masses in order. Can we bear such a prospect?

Have we no love for our country? Is patriotism dead, and is bourgeois morality to prevail, content with growing fat itself, and letting posterity look after itself? Instead of the Creed, shall we chaunt over our steaming tables, 'Let us eat and drink, for to-morrow we die'? Instead of worship and solemn Sacrament, shall the 'dog return to his vomit again and the sow that was washed to her wallowing in the mire'? Then will have come the day—wished for by waiting rivals and races once crushed beneath our power, whose hatred at last begins to sharpen its knife—the day of England's decadence. 'When there is not only no religion among a people, but no belief, when education in the earliest years has relaxed every binding tie by teaching the child to analyse everything remorselessly, that nation is falling to pieces; it is kept together only by the ligatures of material interest, by the laws of that worship which is the offspring of egotism.'[1]

But when men have lost the ideal of God, when the cross of Christ has no voice to their souls, but is a dishonoured gibbet, when injustice fears no future if only in this life it can be secret, and passion knows no mercy, but gluts itself and flings the refuse away, and self-indulgent indolence simpers out, 'Why should I give up for others, I suppose my happiness is as important as theirs?'—when death ends all, and man's last use is to fatten the ground with

[1] Balzac.

his carcase—when, instead of heaven as the end, men have for their ideal to be as the straw trodden down for the dunghill—then, I say, will have come the worship of 'false ideals,' which will work 'deep and ever deeper degeneracy,' until, like the Cities of the Plain, men will be burnt up by their consuming vices. It will not be by the advances of science that Christian faith will be driven from the field. It will be that professing Christians have not believed in the great truths which, with orientation and unction and self-satisfaction, they have confessed. Men who have a conscience and a love for their country will surely ask the question, What can I do to be saved from this commonplace belief whose end is to be 'without God and without hope in the world'?

IX

SHAM IMMORTALITY.

What man is there of you, whom if his son ask bread, will he give him a stone?'—*Matthew* vii. 9.

THE Christian belief in a life beyond the grave has had a powerful influence on those who have held it, and that influence has on the whole been for good. If it has made some men undervalue the present life—a work of difficulty, for in doing so it had to vanquish Nature herself—it has certainly been a consolation in suffering, a strength in toil and danger, an impulse towards moral excellence, and a beauty ever filling the horizon in front of us with the undying radiance of hope. And this is confessed even by those who do not hold the Christian belief. Mill says: 'The beneficial effect of such a hope is far from trifling. It makes life and human nature a far greater thing to the feelings, and gives greater strength as well as greater solemnity to all the sentiments which are awakened in us by our fellow-creatures and by mankind at large. It allays the sense of that irony of Nature which is so painfully felt when we see the exertions and sacrifices of a life culminating in the formation of a wise and noble mind, only to disappear from the world when the time has just arrived at which the world seems about to begin reaping the benefit of it.' Professor Clifford says : ' The conclusion of the matter is that belief in God and in a future life is a source of refined and elevated pleasure to those who can hold it.' Mr. Justice Stephen says: ' But on the whole I think it would be carrying scepticism too far to doubt that an habitual belief in a good God who exercises an influence over human life must be a most powerful motive to virtue, or that it has in fact played in various ways a great part in the government of mankind, even when it has not been coupled with a belief in a future state of conscious existence, and much more when it has.'

Indeed, so much is there in the Christian doctrine of immortality which captivates the imagination and touches the heart, that the apostles of unbelief are constrained to find a substitute for it, and they preach an immortality in words which are anointed with the unction of the pulpit. But all that is true in their doctrine has been a conscious Christian possession, and I may say a human possession, since man became capable of reflection ; and all that is new is the sight of infidelity strutting the highways in garments stolen from Christianity. They teach that the dead live on in those who come after them, that the dead have a real place in succeeding generations and make them what they are, that the dead are the true rulers of the present, and are often more powerful than when they were alive. It is said by Comte, 'The dead more and more control the living.' It is said by Mr. F. Harrison that the dead are to be seen 'not in their mortal past as laid to their rest, but as still living around us and as active as they ever were in life.' And another writer asks, 'Is it not soberly true of a great benefactor of mankind that he has a larger and fuller human life after death than he had when he actually lived? Putting off mortality he puts on immortality;' and he speaks of a dead mother or sister or lover or child 'having a continuing life in us.'[1] Now there is paltering with a double sense in these

> High words that bear
> Semblance of worth, not substance.

The apologists of unbelief, when they say 'the dead are still living around us and are as active as ever they were in life,' do not mean by 'living' what men usually mean. They do not mean that they are living in the sense in which they were said to be living before they died. Indeed they mean by 'living' something quite different. For they do not believe in the immortality of the soul—that is, in the continued existence of the conscious rational being, of that unity we call the ego or self. They do think that death is the loss of the life of consciousness, which most men look upon as the very essence of life,

[1] Dr. Maudsley.

and a loss of that life for ever and ever. 'When, then, we lay our friend in the grave with tears, we do not hope to see his face any more. Be that uncompromisingly admitted.'[1] In this sense it may be said that they believe in annihilation, not of course in the annihilation of the matter of which the body is composed, but they do hold that the 'individual perishes,' if 'the world is more and more.'

This loss for ever of consciousness is terrible for the majority to contemplate. What good is it to tell them that they will be still living after death and as active as ever, if they will not know it, and will not feel it? If they will see nothing, hear nothing, know nothing, will nothing, after death; if they will remember nothing, be interested in nothing, love nothing; if with them it will be the insensibility of a block of ice, a black night, in which no sound is heard, no movement possible for evermore—then to call such a state 'living' is scarcely honest. When my heart is touched by the vision of the dead mother or child, and the ministers of unbelief soothe me by telling me that they are 'living still,'—that they 'have a continuing life in us,' I say there is sophistry in their pious phrases. The dead mother and child, if their life continues in me, do not know it, do not know themselves. I know them—that is, I remember them, I long for them. Oh what would I not give to get them back again! Dear dead ones, why will ye not

[1] Mr. V. Lushington.

speak? But there is no voice. If they are near me, they do not know it. That mother in me has no memory of the day when her pangs lightened into gladness, none of the child-talk sweeter than music to her soul, none of the boy's proud kiss when he promised to be the strength of her widowed years. And is it not but a cruel play upon words to say that that mother is still around us, still lives, and is as active as ever? Is not this but giving a stone to the sorrowful who ask for bread? If the stone is all that we have to give, it is scarcely manly to wrap it up in a tract of the discarded faith and pass it off as the bread of life.

Surely these new teachers are badly off for clothes to dress their doctrines in—shall I not say with which to disguise them? Are there no fig-leaves, æsthetic or scientific, which they can hang upon them that they steal fragments from the robes of Christ? What are we to understand by such a statement as this—'The great benefactor lives a fuller human life after death than he had when he actually lived'? Then I suppose the death of a benefactor of the race is a blessing to mankind, to kill a great benefactor is to make him more effective, and the world has really been wise and beneficent when it has murdered its prophets and stoned them which were sent unto it. But when we are told that 'putting off mortality they put on immortality,' men of gentle feeling, whatever their opinions, rise in rebellion against such a perversion of words already appropriated to a very different purpose.

Cannot materialism go for quotations to its poets of the flesh and its prophets of the earth instead of stealing from psalmist, evangelist, and apostle?

In what sense do the great benefactors of the world put on immortality according to the new Evangel? They themselves, as themselves, ceased for ever to be at the moment they died. Is it that they are had in everlasting veneration by those they have blessed? But the greatest benefactors of the world are unknown to fame. He who, at will, first produced and utilised fire, the first conscious arrangers of words in speech, the makers of alphabets, the domesticators of cattle, the first cultivators of cereals, to say nothing of those chiefs in the march of human progress, the first co-ordinators of religion—these are utterly unknown; like the grave of Moses, no man knoweth them. If they may be said to have put on immortality, it is not that they themselves are immortal, nor that their names are immortal; it is that their discoveries and inventions are immortal. They said something, or they did something, which continues in its effects to the present day. But that is not themselves, any more than Stephenson is the steam-engine or Hargreaves the spinning-jenny. And as for the sacred phrase of the Christian, so rudely appropriated by the unbeliever, it becomes senseless in his hands. He says the great benefactor 'puts off mortality and puts on immortality,' and he means by it that the great work is immortal. But there is no connection between the great benefactor's putting off mortality and his work putting on immortality. The death of an inventor does not make his work immortal. If the man had not put off mortality, if he had gone on living to the years of Methuselah or had never died at all, it would have made no difference to the great work. The work is not the man, and it lives on without regard to him; it lives on its own merits.

These
> raptures conjured up
> To serve occasion of poetic pomp,

simply come to this—Conduct of every kind has its consequences, and these consequences reach to future generations. To quote Mr. Harrison's words: 'There is an indefinite persistence of thoughts and acts and feelings throughout human life, however remote in time; . . . the least of our words and of our thoughts has its own inevitable sequence. It must act on the brain, the heart, the will of others, and so must pass into the immense consensus of life.' This is the substitute for the Christian eternal life—a substitute which we are told is 'real and inspiring.' That our conduct will influence the future is as much a fact and faith to the Christian as it is to the Positivist; whatever 'inspiration' such a fact can give is as much ours as his. The Positivist teacher admits that it was 'shared by Paul and Pascal.' But if there is no other immortality than this, that a man's conduct will continue to have its effects in the future, it is for the greater part of mankind an immortality which is uninspiring, and for many an immortality of hopeless night. If a few great spirits go to the tomb, whose black gates shall never more be opened to let them out, sustained by the thought that succeeding generations will be happier and better because they once lived, how few must they be, and the heaven of Positivism be smaller than that of the most exclusive Calvinism.

How insignificant must be the effect of a single life, such as that lived by thousands and millions of human beings, on the next generation; still less upon that which is more remote, and ever growing smaller and fainter as the ages advance! We may say that a pebble dropped from Dover cliff will have its effect upon the storm-beaten rocks of Cape Horn, but the effect of any one ordinary life upon distant generations, 'however remote in time,' must be smaller still. And when we remember that if every act has its persisting effects, then our bad acts, our silly acts, our mean acts have their effects, their immortality, just as our good ones have—and there cannot be much inspiration in the immortality of our vices and follies. When we remember that the sins of our youth and all our baseness and brutality, the evil spirits we have made guests of in our heart, that 'mob of white-faced thieves' which steals our good resolutions—that these shall be alive and active when we are dead, that they shall be our very selves, 'as living and as active as ever,' this is surely a hell as terrible as any which the dark ages of Christianity ever painted. If this is to be the life to come, we may well wish for a great sword long enough to smite the future, and strong enough to strike off the heads of the offspring which will bear our names. It is said to have been one of Philip of Macedon's maxims of State, 'that whoever puts to death the father must also kill the sons.' I should like to know how the Positivist is to do that.

We are told by one whose modesty at least is never very embarrassing that 'Not all peoples survive and advance, nor all sections of a people, nor all families of a section, nor all individuals of a family; it is only a chosen part, and that a small minority of the whole, which carries forward the progress of humanity; the huge majority is at best stationary and for the most part actually occupied in degenerating.'[1] I ask, What inspiration has this counterfeit immortality for the 'huge majority'? Materialism has no gospel, no glad tidings for the 'huge majority.' It can only say, 'Poor wretches, you are doomed to degenerate. You will live in your successors, a meaner lower life, and then a still lower one, until extinction is happily reached.' Well, that must be very inspiring to the 'huge majority.' But we are told that the same fate may befall the solitary few, who deserve to live, which awaits the 'huge majority.' 'It is not unlikely that natural selection will act to lead mankind downhill at last to their extinction as effectively as it now acts to lead them uphill.'[2]

[1] Dr. Maudsley.   [2] *Ibid.*

And if this should turn out to be true, the fact for great and simple alike to contemplate, the 'common conception still real and inspiring,' is, that we shall have a continuing life in a race, fated in the long run to degrade, until it hears no voice but that of its belly, until it starves, and its cries grow faint and ever fainter, at length to be frozen into silence and eternal death.

I am not to-day engaged in proving the truth of the Christian doctrine of immortality. It may be poetry, illusion, what you will; but anyhow it is something a great deal more elevating and inspiring, than the prospect of possibly being an atom in the shivering carcase of some starved-out last man. It can scarcely sustain the great and good to labour for such a consummation as this, and the poor and the distressed and the bereaved will not grow patient and hopeful, because they may have an unrecognisable part in men still poorer and more miserable. Such teaching is demoralising, and tends to bring about the degradation it contemplates so complacently. In one of Longfellow's letters, written after the tragical death of his wife, he says, 'Did you ever examine what the photographers call the *negative*, on which all that is to be light is dark, and the reverse ? If so, you will feel how beautiful was the remark made by a brother-in-law of mine that this world is only the negative of the world to come, and what is dark here will be light hereafter.' Such was the hope which inspired the spotless, tender spirit of the American poet, and such faith and hope are nourished by the poetry which is dear to the widespread English race. It was more than resignation which sang

> There is no Death ! what seems so is transition ;
> This life of mortal breath
> Is but a suburb of the life Elysian
> Whose portals we call Death.

Lord Beaconsfield once said that the 'poets were the unacknowledged legislators of mankind.' But whether they are the acknowledged or the unacknowledged, we may thank God that they are more potent, in preserving and stimulating faith in God and hope of immortality, than all the unfeeling teachers who, with the recklessness of a savage destroying a work of art no labour of man can re-create, assail these brightest possessions of human life. We cannot listen to the 'scrannel pipes' of materialism, while such sweet music solicits our ears. There is much in this world which, with all our knowledge, we cannot now explain, but the Christian can afford to wait for an explanation. The burdens which oppress him bear down equally upon those who reject his faith, but for them there is no explanation. Life for them must grow darker, until there falls upon them the eternal night. But the religion of Christ can embrace all true philosophy and science, all which appertains to man, and give it a prospect and a hope no human synthesis can supply. It is the promise of 'the life that now is and of that which is to come.'

> Oh welcome, pure-eyed faith, white-handed hope,
> Ye hovering angels girt with golden wings.

X.

ETERNAL PUNISHMENT.

'Knowing therefore the terror of the Lord, we persuade men.'—
2 *Corinthians* v. 11.

WHATEVER the reason may be, men do not now think much about the terror of the Lord, and preachers do not preach much about it. Even our hymns at Advent, which speak of the descending Judge 'robed in dreadful majesty,' and of the ungodly 'filled with guilty fears whose sighs are unavailing,' seem struck in too high a key—at least they do not make the scene stand before us so as to subdue our voices to trembling awe. They are not in accord with the spirit of the present day. That spirit is sceptical. The bold assertions of the past provoke nothing but a gently subdued contempt. Men are now proudly certain of but one thing, and that is that there is nothing of which they can be certain. And this spirit has diffused itself through the abodes of Christian belief. It has diluted it until an uninfluential assent has taken the place of a realistic belief, the fires of faith have been put out and only the grey ashes remain, and the terror of the Lord has become

> A tale of little meaning, though the words are strong.

Again, Christian teachers, in growing numbers, are yielding to the belief that a day will come when sin shall for ever cease, when the works of the Devil shall be destroyed, 'that God may be all in all.' These men are said not to believe in eternal punishment. Now, whether they are right or wrong in believing that sin shall all be washed away from the world by the blood of Christ, and the chaff burnt up by the fires of His Holy Spirit which man shall never be able to quench, I think they are misunderstood. They do not believe in *eternal sin*; but whether certain consequences of sin may not be everlasting they have not so clearly determined. What they affirm is the article of the Apostles' Creed, 'I believe in the forgiveness of sins,' the article of the Nicene Creed, 'I believe in one baptism for the remission of sins.' But, since there can be no remission of sins while sins are being committed, they believe that sins will cease to be committed, for there is no other remission of sins than this. A state of sin is a state of enmity with God, and as long as a state of sin continues, a state which is enmity with God continues. Enmity with God can only cease when sin ceases. We need not, however, fasten upon them the belief that the punishment of sin is not enduring; the two beliefs do not necessarily go together.

But many of us, whose faith if not vivid is yet what is called sound, are in danger of perverting that great article of Christian belief, the remission of sins; and the spirit of profligacy does pervert it, and the spirit of moral vulgarity perverts it, and the spirit of cowardly improvidence longs to have it so. The perversion is, that the punishment of sin is to be remitted, that the forgiveness of sins practically means letting us off from the penalty of our sins, that it is going to be all right whatever we do, that there is no hell, and that men may make themselves quite comfortable, for there is nothing in the future to fear. Now against all this the Christian teacher must never cease to protest, for it is a great lie; it is a flat contradiction to the laws of nature. Whether we believe that, in very literal truth, the Lamb of God will take away the sin of the world, and that Jesus Christ's coming to save sinners will be completely effective; or whether we believe that evil will last as long as the throne of God, that from the pit its black incense of curses will for ever ascend; one thing is certain, that there is no remission of the punishment of sin. The saint must bear his punishment, and the impenitent sinner ever augment his. God is not the feeble, good-natured God of languid or frivolous profligacy. The words of the Bible have terrible truth in them: 'God is righteous and awful and full of vengeance.' In one sense He is unmerciful and unrelenting. We have to do with unaltering design and intention, and with irresistible power. You may better argue with a Nasmyth's hammer as it falls, or murmur dulcet words of peace to the thundering avalanche, than interfere with the retribution which is inseparable from sin. The punishment of sin according to the constitution of Nature, which simply means the mind and will of God, is certain, and often instantaneous and enduring. You ask me, Do I believe in eternal punishment? I answer, I do—albeit the words *eternal punishment* may not convey to me precisely the same meaning which they do to you. I cannot believe in anything else. At least I can put before my mind the thought of punishment outliving sin, because I see that it does so day by day before my eyes; because I see that, in a very solemn sense, all punishment is eternal. I can conceive the punishment of sin as being, in one sense, necessarily everlasting, if too often we have misunderstood the law and nature of that punishment.

What is sin? The Bible has given us an exact answer, ' Sin is the transgression of the law.' The great law of existence is, Conform to the conditions of existence. Whether men believe in God or not, they will admit that. If a man will not take food, or leaps over a precipice, or daily poisons himself with alcohol or opium, God or no God, the punishment is certain, and may never be removed. The law of existence is, Conform to the conditions of existence or perish. But I will lift this thought into a higher realm, and will say that from the conditions of existence God cannot be excluded; that if we must conform to the conditions of existence we must conform to God; that the ultimate and highest law of existence is, 'Be ye reconciled to God.' Now if we do not conform to the conditions of existence we must in time cease to exist. Whether the conditions of existence we ignore, be bodily or mental, or moral or spiritual, from that moment we begin to destroy our physical, mental, moral, and spiritual life. And so the words spoken to primitive man—one of the earliest revelations made to him, a warning by which his life might be saved—were, 'In the day thou eatest thereof thou shalt surely die.' The law is inexorable. It says, Only on certain conditions may you live. If you do not conform I will kill you, slowly or quickly I will kill you. You shall smart and suffer in the process of dissolution, and the pain may check you and stop you and turn you back into the way of law, which in fact is the way of righteousness. 'The law of Nature,' says an Agnostic writer on Ethics, 'has but one precept, "Be strong." Nature has but one punishment, decay culminating in death or extirpation; and takes cognisance of but one evil, the weakness which leads to decay.'[1]

It is the fashion now to condemn the divines and preachers of other days for their fervid assertions of the consequences of sin. I myself have followed the fashion. It is quite possible, and I think quite certain, that they misunderstood the nature and law of Divine punishment. But they did feel the awful solemnity

[1] Mr. Leslie Stephen.

of human conduct, and their wildest denunciations were at least more respectable than the frivolous Epicureanism which seems to say, 'Oh yes, there is a very good God, and there is no need to be apprehensive or alarmed. He will not punish men for their little follies and the faults of human nature.' And is that the God who is set upon the throne of the universe ? — a God like some feeble, profligate monarch, too old to do much harm himself, but who did not mind it in other people. Does anyone mean that that is the God to whom he says his prayers? We should be too manly to bow to such a being. A faith of that kind will in the long run take every bit of moral fibre out of a man. It will reduce his character to a boneless pulp and his worship to a mindless posture. It was said by Mr. Maurice, 'The barest Utilitarianism which is in earnest is better than a Sentiment and a Religion which are only an excuse for self-indulgence and contempt.' And I will say, infinitely nobler is the stern God of Calvinism than the Grand Monarque of religious indifferentism.

Even science has a better God. If the God of the Christian is a languid Eli who only shakes his head condoningly over the excesses of his children, the God of the materialist, Nature, knows how to avenge. If we cannot speak of the terror of the Lord, science can fulminate the terrors of the Law. Indeed it is surprising how fierce some of the new teachers, who ignore Christianity, are becoming. They catch up the tones of the old threatening prophets. The authorised preachers of churches and chapels have forgotten to denounce. They have eaten the lotus of scepticism, and the old threats which once raged around them now seem 'to mourn and rave on alien shores;' but science has her Boanerges who thunder out damnation. What we used to call *perdition*, when we had the use of our tongue, they call 'extirpation and natural elimination.' But I do not think that to be 'extirpated' or 'naturally eliminated' can be a very pleasant kind of thing. It does not seem to me to differ much from what we used to call *destruction*. Here is an instance in which words of the Bible even are appropriated by an anti-Christian writer: 'There is, so to speak, a broad and easy way leading to degeneration, decay and death, which is the opposite of the steep and narrow path that leads to evolution and fuller life.' And here is a threat of punishment, which we may almost call a threat of everlasting punishment, once uttered by a brilliant, unbelieving mathematician,[1] who now knows more of the unseen land than the sons of the living: 'He who stifles his own doubts or hampers the inquiry of others is guilty of a sacrilege which centuries shall never be able to blot out. When the labours and questionings of honest and brave men shall have built up the fabric of known truth to a glory which we in this generation can neither hope for nor imagine, in that pure and

[1] Professor Clifford.

holy temple he shall have no part nor lot, but his name and his works shall be cast into the darkness of oblivion for ever.' Positivism has also its doctrine of eternal destruction. Although it says, 'There is for us no heaven, no hell, no other world,' it still maintains that there is 'for us, if we be worthy, a life after death.' It is true that life after death is a life in Humanity. But that life is not for all, it is only for those who are 'worthy.' The 'unworthy ones form no part of Humanity.'[1] In other words, there is no life for 'unworthy ones' after death, and Positivism has its dogma of eternal destruction.

Well, it all comes to this, that men cannot bear for long the softened voices of Lotus-land. Nature forbids it; she begins to murmur and threaten and thunder. If old preachers and painters and poets were too lurid in their materialistic representations, Nature says, This is no place of irresponsible dalliance, it is a place of unrelenting punishment. Look at the broken shattered beings who stagger on until they collapse into a grave. Those bright wild days when they were strong and defied results have wrought their revenge. You say, It was more thoughtlessness or pique or daring than real badness of heart. Yes, perhaps it was, but that did not save them. It may be that they have passed away to some strange land to conceal their shame—never more to take the place to which they were born—or to the grave ere manhood had been

[1] Mr. V. Lushington.

fully reached. Every sin against your body has some instant punishment. Every sin is a step to death. No praying will stop it. God's law must be fulfilled, and so it is written, 'Be sure your sins will find you out. . . . His bones are full of the sin of his youth, which shall lie down with him in the dust.'

> Riches we wish to get,
> Yet remain spendthrifts still;
> We would have health, and yet
> Still use our bodies ill;
> Bafflers of our own prayers from youth to life's last scenes.
>
> We would have inward peace,
> Yet will not look within;
> We would have misery cease,
> Yet will not cease from sin;
> We want all pleasant ends, but will use no harsh means;
>
> We do not what we ought,
> What we ought not, we do,
> And lean upon the thought
> That chance will bring us through;
> But our own acts, for good or ill, are mightier powers.'

Sin is always a process of self-destruction, and its most fearful consequences are upon the moral and spiritual nature itself. Its first effect is pain, the pain inflicted by conscience when wrong has been consciously done. Oh happy pains of saving, arresting conscience! Oh miserable, hopeless state when conscience has been stupefied, and we go with light heart to the sin which has done the deed, and will soon complete our destruction! For if every act

¹ Mr. M. Arnold.

of man is registered in his body, so that in some part of his frame each act has left its trace, like a subtle poison or disease whose effects cannot be expelled from the tissues—if now even from our bodies the tale of our most secret sin could be extracted—so too our sins, that is, as conscious breaches of moral and divine law, are all registered in the spiritual nature. No single act can be lost. It is all marked into the being. It has been said that 'In the living present the incorporate past is active;' and, again, 'The conscious motives of past years are incorporated structurally as unconscious factors in the motives of to-day;' and as the Ninth Article declares 'the infection of nature doth remain in them that are regenerate.' Amid the million experiences we have undergone, each single one, in some form, under some modification or other, is there, and the tests of the All-seeing can show the stain. That lie, that lust, that cowardly cruelty, that self-seeking hypocrisy, all that thou hast done has made its mark on thee, has made thee something other than thou mightest have been. On the unseen face which stands behind thine eyes, every sin has marked its line; leaving a bewildering confusion, like the labyrinth of veins and nerves and reticulations betrayed when the skin is removed.

Remember, for God's sake, we can never make that to be undone which once we have done. Omnipotence cannot do it. The blood of Christ cannot do it. *It can wash out the guilty taint,* but the fact must remain a fact about us for evermore. Is not that a punishment? Is not that an eternal punishment? If memory remains to us in the world unseen, whenever that deed, which it may be we now hate and would give worlds not to have done, comes to mind, to human seeming it would appear that pain must arise. Perhaps the Divine vision will so fill the enraptured spirit that nothing will be able to bring back the guilty past to memory. But this part of the punishment may well be named eternal, a punishment for the saint and even for an apostle like St. Peter, that each sin we have committed will be a fact about us nor time nor eternity shall wash away.

But, again, every sin will have this punishment, that it will entail a lower place in the Kingdom of Heaven than we might have had. Sin cannot be a thing of indifference. It must be worse with us to have sinned than not to have sinned. It must be worse with St. Peter that he denied His Lord, than if he had not denied Him; otherwise sin would be a thing indifferent. If I lose time I can never make that up. If it be said, 'Oh yes, by greater work and special effort the lost may be regained.' No! no! If we are capable of what we call greater effort, we could have put forth that greater effort even if we had not lost that time. In this case we should have made still greater progress. If, for instance, we have by sinful indulgence deeply ingrained in our souls evil desires, it will take long to erase them. As men know by bitter experience, they have to watch and wrestle and pray without ceasing to hold back desires which, by indulgence in the past, have grown strong. They have, as it were, day by day to rub down the deep engraving, and only by slow degrees will it become fainter and begin to disappear. *It can disappear and the stain be washed away*; but all the time and power spent in simply undoing the past might have been used to lift the soul into higher heavenly communion, and the soul has lost a place which otherwise it might have had. Every act in this way has its everlasting consequences, every bad act its own unending effect.

And so, again, there is what we may call eternal perdition—something lost never to be found again. The opportunity lost or misimproved to-day is an eternal perdition. You say, you will make up for it to-morrow. But perhaps you cannot make up for it to-morrow, or you may have no to-morrow; or, if you have, you might have done something else to-morrow. There is real, irremediable loss, an eternal perdition. 'Every day in which some line of God's Image is not traced on your souls,' says Dr. Pusey, '*is a loss for eternity.*' Some of our saddest self-reproaches are that we did not do what we ought to have done or as much or as tenderly as we ought to have done when the day was ours, and now the night has come when no man can work. The days indeed are solemn. I have not said one word of hellish flames, or curses from sinful souls never to be silenced.

We do not so much express ourselves in that way now. It is archaic, but facts are changeless. I have been speaking of a law of nature whose operation can be seen around us and is felt within us—a law which must be recognised and obeyed as much by the unbeliever as by the Christian—and it is that each day will live, in some way or other enregistered in the living being, as long as that being shall exist. I will not quote the words of divines to enforce what I deeply feel. 'It is much to get rid of superstition,' says a recent writer on philosophy, ' it is much to be quit of the notions of Hell and Devil ; possibly it is of still greater ethical value to know that *sin is never remediable, that Nature never forgives.*'[1] Take these words of Mr. Carlyle which declare the eternal punishment I dare not deny : ' The finger lies on the pistol ; but the man is not yet a murderer—one slight twitch of a muscle, the death-flash bursts ; and he is it, and will for Eternity be it, and Earth has become a penal Tartarus for him ; his horizon girdled now not with golden hope, but with red flames of remorse ; voices from the depths of Nature, sounding Wo, wo on him.' And no less solemn are the words of Mr. Ruskin : ' Wisdom never forgives. Whatever resistance we have offered to her law she avenges for ever ; the lost hour can never be redeemed, and the accomplished wrong never atoned for. The best that can be done afterwards, but for that, had been better. The falsest of all the cries of

[1] Mr. Courtenay.

peace, where there is no peace, is that of the pardon of sin, as the mob expect it. Wisdom can "put away sin," but she cannot pardon it, and she is apt, in her haste, to put away the sinner as well, when the black ægis is on her breast.' And now, whatever scepticism may say, and whatever sentimental religionism may say, this is what in her own way science says, and this is what the Bible says, 'Be not deceived, God is not mocked, for whatsoever a man soweth that shall he reap.'

XI.

NEED OF SALVATION.

'Without Me ye can do nothing.'—*St. John* xv. 5.

ONE of the most fundamental dogmas of Evangelical Christianity is that we cannot save ourselves, that no man can save his own soul; and one of our Church Collects asserts, without qualification of any kind, the doctrine of human insufficiency. It says, 'Almighty God, who seest that we have no power of ourselves to help ourselves.' Now this teaching has always been an offence to those who are full of energy and courage and ambition, and it certainly seems to be in opposition to plain facts. We are disposed to ask, Cannot a man who determinately tries to be better succeed in being better? Cannot a man who struggles continuously against some evil sooner or later get the mastery over it? We feel sure that he can. If by saving the soul be meant saving it from the dominion of evil habits, and if a man struggle incessantly by all the means in his power to break down the stronghold of evil habit, then we are certain that a man can do much to save his soul, and that it is his duty to obey the command, 'Work out your own salvation.' And yet such a saying as I have quoted from the Collect, 'We have no power of ourselves to help ourselves,' such a cry as that of St. Paul, 'Oh, wretched man that I am, who shall deliver me from the body of this death?' such confessions of spiritual insufficiency and impotency as crowd the pages of Evangelical pietism, do point to a profound truth of human nature, which must be admitted alike by materialist and spiritualist. If by free will we mean freedom to do anything whatever, then there is very little free will in the world.

It is clear enough, when we look at humanity at large, that we are hedged round by barriers which no trying can overleap. No free will can convert the Hindoo character into the Scandinavian, or the Teutonic into the Celtic. The fibre of national character comes as a fate, a destiny which may not be lifted off. And equally true is it of individual character. No amount of willing can turn the dull, dogged nature into one of eager, trembling sensibility. You cannot make the children of the same parents, whose education has been identical, alike in nature. There is no freedom in the matter. You may direct different natures to the same ends, and you may gradually bring about changes in character, but certain differences of quality cannot be overleaped. The atoms of character are unchangeable. Their arrangements may be infinitely varied. You look with regret, with disappointment, on the career of one for whom you expected such very different things; but you see that it cannot be helped, that every movement, every look, every occupation, every pleasure shows you a kind of nature which could not become what you intended. It would require a change which the laws of nature make impossible. There are some people who are essentially common, in whose every taste and pursuit you see a common mind; and you know that if some new cause, or subject, or career, or pleasure offers itself, they will instinctively choose the least refined, the least magnanimous. You can never make miry clay into fine gold. You may make a useful vessel out of the clay, and you may turn the gold to a base use, but one will be common and the other fine. 'Which of you by taking thought can add one cubit to his stature?'

Look at the victims of certain vices. You do not say there is no hope, but you think there is very little, and at length the conviction may grow upon you that there is none at all. Those who have much to do with criminals look upon some as absolutely hopeless. They may be well conducted in gaol, and listen to the teachings of the chaplain, and express remorse, and promise amendment; and yet the trained observer will be sure that, on the first opportunity, the thief will be a thief again. There are some men who seem to be utterly incapable of speaking the truth. Their first feeling is a shrinking from speaking the plain truth. Even when no interest is served by falsehood, it seems to come easier to them, and more natural to them, to be untrue than to be true. This vice seems to pursue them through life. Those who know them always mistrust them. They do not expect from them any sudden exertion of what is called free will; they do not think it as likely that they will speak the truth as that they will lie. They know their nature as they know their appearance, and expect to find each unchanged. The case of drunkenness is too plain to need illustration. The mean, ungenerous miserly nature rarely undergoes serious and permanent modification, and the coward seldom acquires a steady and constant courage. I do not say that these diseases are never cured, indeed I want to show the only way by which men can be saved from them; but I do say that the sphere in which we are absolutely self-competent is a comparatively small one, and that many things are quite impossible for us. It is written down in our nature as an ordinance for ever, *Thou* at least shall not be that, and many other things for thee must be extremely difficult. I do not say that a man cannot do what he wills to do. On the contrary, I am sure he can. 'Good intention,' says Emerson, 'clothes itself with sudden power.' That is the true signification of free will. What we will, we can do, unless we are coerced or restrained by some external power mightier than ourselves. Yes—an act is done, as far as the soul is concerned, when a man has willed it. The will is the whole mind in action, the resultant of the mind's various and conflicting energies. Acts of will are the supreme moments of life.

But some men cannot will certain things, at least they cannot of themselves; they can like, and wish, and long, and sigh for them.

> I can intend up to a certain point,
> No further.[1]

Only a power external to themselves can compress them into an act of will. In such cases salvation must be by a power outside ourselves. It is true that we have 'no power of ourselves to help ourselves.' For a man can only act in accordance with his character. He does not stand apart from his character so that he can say, Now I will act according to my character and now I will act in opposition to my character. Every act is equally a product of character. Character is self. It is that nature of ours which shows itself in our disposition and mode of conduct. Voluntary conduct is the outside of character, and character is the inside of conduct. They cannot be separated; one implies the other. If a man did not act in accordance with his character, then he must act in accordance with somebody else's character—in fact be somebody else, which is impossible. A man's character at this moment is a positive fact. You are this minute what you are, and your conduct this minute must be in accordance

[1] Mr. Browning.

with what you are; it cannot be in accordance with anything else.

But when I say you must act in accordance with your character, I do not say you will always perform the same act whatever be the circumstances; but that in all circumstances, however various, you must act according to your nature—that you are you and only you. A ruffian may despoil the dead on the night of a battle, and for plunder may murder the wounded who are unable to defend themselves. There is the opportunity—what we call temptation—and there is the character. The act is certain. But change the circumstances. The skulking cowardly robber and assassin, as he peers around for his prey, sees the lights and hears the steady tramp of soldiers who come to save the wounded and to bury the dead; and, like some foul night-bird gorging on the slaughtered, the miscreant glides away from the spoil he covets and the doom he deserves. He acted in accordance with his character when he ventured upon the battle-field and when he fled. You may see a man in the goodly company of virtue and religion, where purity of manners and loftiness of temper and piety of soul charm with their fascinating converse, and the man seems to be in his proper place and to move in a becoming attitude. None could think him an intruding impostor. And yet the same man, in another company, speaks ribald jests, and hums the airs of dissipation, and knows not how pitiful is the swagger of irreverence. The miserable creature's character was the same, though the conduct was so different. Some comfort or sustenance was needed, which braggart license could not give, and a part was acted where the real nature dared not show itself. The man had one vice more than we have recounted, and that was hypocrisy. Or it may be that the character was utterly weak, reflecting everything put before it; good feelings were really present when the air was pure, and the man was not quite so bad in heart as he seemed to be when vulgar vice was around him.

A man must be himself at each moment of his life. We ask a character before we employ a man, because we expect that his future conduct will accord with his past conduct. Sometimes even one fault clings to a man through life in its disastrous consequences. Men take the fault to be the index of the character, and though years have gone by since the fault was committed, people feel as though he might do it again—they feel as if it were in him. The noble characters of some men leave them no freedom to do evil. They could not do that base thing. The triumph of Divine grace in the soul determines the character and blocks the way to badness. 'We regard it as the problem which education has to solve, that not merely the trifling movements to which the incidents of every-day life give rise, but, further, our whole moral conduct should appear as the involuntary expression of a noble nature, free from the melancholy seriousness of deliberate purpose, and therefore free from any thought of being able to be different.'[1] The repulsion which virtue has for vice is seen in the lofty patriarchal saying, 'How can I do this great wickedness and sin against God?' 'A good man out of the good treasure of his heart bringeth forth good things, and an evil man out of the evil treasure of his heart bringeth forth evil things. A good tree cannot bring forth evil fruit, neither can a corrupt tree bring forth good fruit.'

But may not character change? Because a man is bad this minute, must he always remain bad? Is there a stern, absolute fate in human life, and is an iron Calvinism the only resting-place for the perplexed spirit? Not only may character change—I believe it is changing every minute. But change implies a cause. A thing must remain the same if there is nothing to change it. A change cannot rise up spontaneously, without any reason, antecedent, or cause. When naturalists talk of spontaneous variations and sports and so forth, they only mean that the variations are of a kind whose cause is too remote or obscure for them to discover. There is no more spontaneous variation than there is spontaneous generation. Sports are as impossible as chance. Each has an adequate, if as yet undiscovered, cause. Every variation is a reaction of some kind or other; it is the result of some change which we call a cause. If

[1] Lotze.

a change occurs in character, it is the result of some change outside of character. Change comes on change. No man, without any reason whatever, can in a moment determine to change his character from bad to good, still less can he in a moment do it.

And yet men have in a moment come to a determination and at once set about its accomplishment; and the usual explanation is that a call from God, some hidden action of the Divine mind upon the human mind, was the cause of the sudden conversion. And it is easy to see that if, for instance, a direct call from God could pierce through some bad man's soul, if some heavenly fascination could act upon it, some awful view of the deeps of evil could alarm it, then such a change from without a man, could make a change within a man and be a new point of departure. But this is a transcendent realm of which we can affirm little. Such a conversion as that of St. Paul is beyond our investigation. It is too mysterious for our analysis, and its law too remote for our reckoning. 'The wind bloweth where it listeth, and thou hearest the sound thereof, and canst not tell whence it cometh and whither it goeth; so is every one that is born of the Spirit.'

But there are ways of Divine activity more on a level with our comprehension—the ordinary, natural, established ways by which God acts upon the minds and souls of His children, in all of whom there is that presence of the Holy Spirit which is man's potentiality of salvation. If there were no other way than the transcendent way—the way, as it were, of sudden miracle—then we could do nothing but wait for the miracle, the uncertain troubling of the water. If there were no means of salvation but the supernatural, incalculable voice of God, then men could do nothing but wait till the Spirit moved them. Man could not help his fellows; each must sit apart expecting if perchance a call should come to him, one being taken and another left. This is not all. There is salvation for man by man, and this as God's verified law. On this law I must hereafter discourse. But the Son of Man is come to seek and to save that which was lost. Men need not be left in pining uncertainty, waiting for a secret voice, if only those who know the truth will cry aloud to all they meet, Come unto the marriage, for the doors are open and all things are now ready.

XII.

MEANS OF SALVATION.

'Brethren, if any of you do err from the truth, and one convert him, let him know, that he which converteth the sinner from the error of his way shall save a soul from death, and shall hide a multitude of sins.'—*St. James* v. 19, 20.

IN the previous sermon I made some remarks upon the ever-perplexing subject of the freedom of the will. It was for a practical purpose I did so, not for one moment imagining that I was contributing anything to the solution of problems which have defied human thought for centuries. But we found that the Bible and our Prayer-Book alike declared that man, of his own unaided self, cannot rise from his natural condition to newness of life—in Evangelical phrase, cannot save his own soul; and that the facts of human nature said very much the same thing. We are pressed upon and shut in by humanity and by nationality. We are free corpuscles in a great body whose larger life controls and uses our activities. Yet have we individual life as well as corporate. We are carried about, and yet at the same time we move freely in our little sphere. It will not help the superficial sceptic of society to do away with the hard facts of human nature, because he makes merry over religious phrases, and jauntily declares that he is a free man and can do what he likes. The profound materialist, no less than the unaccommodating Calvinist, knows full well that our conduct is limited by our nature; and though we may mean somewhat different things by the ' saving of the soul,' yet it is true for both that man needs a Saviour.

For, as I endeavoured to show, there is no freedom of the will to act in opposition to the nature. It is not the will which rules the nature, but the nature which expresses itself in the will. Your will and your nature or character are not two separate things. Your will is a part of your nature and cannot be separated from it. You may say ' you could do things if you liked, but that you would not.' Precisely— ' if you liked.' But it is because you do not like that you do not do them. To say you could do a thing, only you would not, is a flat contradiction. You mean that, if it were not for the strong feeling you have on the subject, the mere act would be quite easy. But the strong feeling which would not let you do that thing is *you*; it is your character which makes that act impossible. You must act in accordance with your character. A bad man will act badly, and a religious man religiously. 'The willing is the doing in this case; and he that says he is willing to do his duty, but he cannot, does not understand what he says.'[1]

[1] Bishop Taylor.

Now if this were all, each must go his fated way to heaven or hell, and the gospel of salvation be an impotent dream. But we do see that character changes; the common experiences of life show it; we have seen bad men become good men, and common souls bowed down in worship. Let us see what character consists of, and then we may possibly see where, and in what way, it may be changed. First of all there is that character we bring with us into this world, which we call our nature. And then there is that second nature which education and habit impart. Christian divines in all times have taught that man comes into this world with a decided character, bent, or bias. They call it human depravity, and they account for it by original sin. And modern science is equally strong in maintaining that man comes into this world with the shaping influence of the past upon him, and a depravity inherited from savage or animal ancestors. Anyhow, here is the fact, a man comes into the world a positive and decided kind of being, with a nature of a fixed quality and texture; a nature which is a kind of concrete, a fusing together of all sorts of broken fragments and dust of the past; or, to take a more living illustration, a soil with all sorts of buried seeds in it. Which will grow depends altogether upon circumstances.

Now I am on the whole inclined to think that this first nature is the nature which is capable of least alteration, in some respects of none at all.

'Nature,' says Lord Bacon, 'is often hidden, sometimes overcome, seldom extinguished.' And yet, within this first nature may frequently be found the means of making an alteration in character. Often you do not know what is in a man, he does not know what is in himself. Parts of his character have never been called into play; there may be seeds there which have never had the chance of growing.

Now we know quite well that one faculty or passion in a man may quite overpower another, and set in motion a totally new activity. You may see a man, who seems to have no aim in life, who does not know what to do, who finds life almost a burden, or who drags on his monotonous daily work cursing its dulness. But the seed of love is quickened in his soul, the happy blood of honourable passion warms his brain and braces his muscles; he has an object, he must win a competence or lay some prize and honour at the feet of the beloved. The seed long hidden grows into a tree, and the tree grows until it occupies the whole ground which once was filled with other growths, and beneath its shade they dwindle or die. So, alas! is it that we see some one for whom we felt respect and regard fall into a baseness or a crime. There was a bad seed in the character which none knew anything about; but the ploughshare of life brought it near the surface, and then it started into growth. Again to quote Lord Bacon, 'Nature will lie buried a great time, and yet revive upon the occasion or temptation.'

Now this first inherited nature, which, as I incline to think, cannot in its substance be changed, may be variously employed, and by means of one element in it another may be controlled.

Then there is the second nature, that which has been formed by habit. This nature is, as we may say, accidental, not essential—that is, it might have been different. The same natural texture of character might have been worked up into other forms and shaped for other purposes. Circumstances took up the texture and made it what it is. Now, since this character, this second nature, is a formation in time, it may be unformed in time; the habit which came of continuous single acts, by continuous single acts may be destroyed. In the superimposed character there is room for the very greatest change. You may change the building ever so much, if you cannot change the materials out of which it is built. The inherited natural character is the material; education, circumstances, build the house. You may build a palace, a shop, a hovel, a retreat of infamy; but if the natural character be brick or stone or marble or mud, so likewise will be the structure.

Here, then, we see the two constituents of character, each of which in its own way may be the subject of change, the one indirectly and the other directly. But what can set up a change? Change cannot come of itself. Uncaused change is an absurdity. Let the very same character, absolutely unaltered, be placed again and again in precisely the same circumstances, and the conduct must be the same, for there is nothing to make it different. But, even if the character does remain the same, we know that change in circumstances will alter the conduct. The drunkard who could not reject a glass of spirits freely offered to him, would refuse to drink it if it were put to his mouth at boiling-point. A man who would steal a jewel would not put out his hand to take it, if he saw that his hand would be caught and crushed in some vice-like trap. There are things of various kinds which people would not do if some one were looking at them. Conduct is ever being changed by circumstances.

But conduct in the long run modifies character, especially that product of habit which we call *second nature*. By some means or other you keep a man from a certain kind of conduct. Every time he is going to do it you tell him of it, you keep an eye upon him so that he cannot get the secrecy he wishes. He would do it, but he has no chance. He is ashamed, he dares not. But abstinence diminishes desire. The longer he continues to refrain from indulgence the less difficult does restraint become. By not doing a thing for a time, a man cares less about doing it; his health is better, his courage higher, his pleasure with others increased, his self-respect more ample. The old taste begins to decay. A joyful audacity fills the eyes which once had a suspicious, hunted look. New habits and tastes are gradually formed. In other words, a new character arises from changed circumstances, from a changed condition of things.

And, again, you want, by means of one part of the primitive character, to bring about a change in the whole character. There may be qualities and capabilities in the character of which you are totally ignorant. If the circumstances, which so far have been unable to bring such qualities to the surface, remain unchanged, they never will come to the surface. But a man may see something, a grace, a beauty he never saw before. He may have known nothing but low company, and been thought incapable of anything better. But his lot is changed, and grace and purity and sympathy and generosity take such fascinating hold of him that he cannot leave them; nay, he fears that they may rather turn away from him. How horrible that past was! How could he have done it! How could he have lived in it! Did he ever really endure such things? Was it not an unpleasant dream? Whether you wish to destroy habit, or by means of one native power to overthrow another, humanly speaking it must be by change of circumstances. Leave men, in all which surrounds them and acts upon them, in precisely the same state, without the smallest change, and they must remain the same. They must be brought into contact with new powers, new saving forces, if they are to be renewed in the spirit of their minds. But since they cannot change themselves, but must be what they are, change must be thrust upon them, their salvation must be directly set up by a power outside themselves. They need a Saviour. This is the Divine Law, and its great manifestation was the Son of God who was Son of Man, who is the perfect illustration of God's dealings with man, the 'fulness of the Godhead bodily.' He came to men who without Him must have remained dead in trespasses and sins, and started them from the grave into newness of life.

And by the same method God still carries on His saving purposes for mankind. Christ is the Head and Model. And still it is true that man must be saved by man. From time to time there appear men who likewise may be called Saviours, for they have put on the Lord Jesus Christ—men of such strong moral and religious power that they take their fellow-men and work wonders of conversion in their souls. These are the special apostles of an age, a nation, or a Church. The law of their appearance we know not. Moral and religious genius is as incalculable as are all other manifestations of genius, yet are all alike in accordance with the Divine Law. Nor is the work confined to these. It is laid upon all whose minds are moved by the sins and sorrows of the world around, it is laid upon all who know that the vices of the world should be strangled in the cradle. An infant is born with a living germ of character whose kind is fixed. It is shaped and formed by circumstances; by parents, brothers, sisters, servants, sights, sounds, indeed by all which in any way reaches the mind. Awful shaping time, that time of infancy and youth! Alas! how terribly hard to undo the work! You want a man to change. It is your husband, your friend, the people committed to your charge. You must act upon them by all the means in your power, intentionally, continuously, even if it be by force. You must act upon them by persuasion, by reason, by love, by noble example. Your manner of life may be a heavenly blessing coming down upon those with whom you work or live. That bad man may have no power at this moment to change to good. But, it may be, a thought, a word, a look, a gesture of yours may set up a change, and a new agency come into power, and a revolution begin, until the old man passes away, and all things become new. One drop of moisture in a body may start a whole world into life in that which before was dead and dry. One word from the pulpit may touch a hidden spring, and the water of life begin to flow. Then 'compel them to come in.'

The evils of the world are great, and the days may be coming when unredressed wrongs will become earthquakes, shattering the mansions of wealth and improvidence. Is there nothing for us to do, no changes in the social and religious condition of our fellow-men which it were wise to bring about? Is there nothing we can do to create healthy homes, to spread education, to diffuse good will, to save men's souls? I cannot tell you in what particular way you should act. You ought not to have a Director. Men must walk alone. But it may be that God wills, through my voice, to start in you the saving change, or turn you into a Saviour. There is the pestilence of evil which is killing men. Are you spreading the poison which lays men in the dust? May God stop you in your evil course! Or do you carry the medicine which revives the soul? Then be sure, oh faithful spirit, that 'he which converteth a sinner from the error of his ways shall save a soul from death, and shall hide a multitude of sins.'

XIII.

SPIRITUAL DEPRESSION.

'Who is among you that feareth the Lord, that obeyeth the voice of his servant, that walketh in darkness, and hath no light? let him trust in the name of the Lord, and stay upon his God.'—*Isaiah* 1.10.

WHATEVER may have been the purpose with which these words were written, they are so full of wisdom that the time will never come when they will cease to convey the secret of peace. I have found them most useful, and especially in the visitation of the sick. For it happens, at times, that those we have known well as gentle Christian souls, whose lives have been the modest embodiments of all Christian graces, are troubled with doubts and fears; they are not sure that they are right in the sight of God; as they say, they do not feel ready to die, they are not sure that they will go to heaven. Their bed of sickness is made hard and uneven by religious restlessness; or in health they have to envy the lot of some who are so confident and bright, whilst they are the victims of depression. Now I have said this text-verse to many a sufferer, because a text has an influence which a conclusive argument very often has not.

There is a charm in a text, whilst a demonstration may be dreary, for the text is a voice to the heart. It will be a long time before the power of the Bible is done away with. Mock as men may at 'Mesopotamias,' at any rate the new religions cannot create them. Bring out the consoling sacred texts from the Bibles of the new Gods, the words which impart new life. Let the Great Being, Humanity, speak through his prophet. Let the Unknowable address us in a saving word from the Synthetic Philosophy. Will they be a charm in the ears of the dying? What sentence of theirs will spring to solemn lips, and speak as from a heavenly land? Where will they get their 'Mesopotamias'? Their doctrines are dry and sterile,—arid steppes which may be surveyed if you carry with you the bread by which a man may live,—but incapable of supporting life. And until they have words which are eternal as the heavens and refreshing as their showers, they can never bring salvation to man.

In other words, science can never be religion. However clear and accurate and comprehensive and illuminating Synthetic Philosophies and Positive Polities may be, and however fabulous and uncritical and unscientific the Bible may be, it can simply laugh all its competitors to scorn. What is their wisdom, their logic, their analysis? What are their weights and scales and measures and decompositions and demonstrations? Simply not powerful enough to rob men, even for a day, of a single text. Religion has to do with that side of the mind's activity which we call the soul, and nothing but that which reaches the soul, or is adapted to its needs, can be called religion; and the stupidest superstition which yet answers to the cry of the soul will be more prized and more powerful than all the books of Euclid or the most accurate biographies of the oyster and the ape. Music, art, poetry, religion are all the responses of the soul of man to facts external to himself, and religion is the greatest of these responses because it is the response of the soul to the voice of God.

The texts of the Bible are inspired by religion. And so I have found this text of mine to-day a blessing to the suffering; for it is inspired with religion, and at the same time it is an instruction as rational as it is religious. It recognises the fact that really good people may yet be enveloped in gloom, and it tells them how to find relief. Experience has shown us that really good people are often uncertain about their religious state and prospects, and reason does show us that calm reliance on the Eternal, in the midst of darkness, will assuage the tumult of the spirit and strengthen the trembling soul. And therefore I have rejoiced in my text, and murmured in the ears of many a sick and fainting and self-distrusting spirit, 'Who is among you that feareth the Lord, that obeyeth the voice of His servant, that walketh in darkness, and hath no light? let him trust in the name of the Lord, and stay upon his God.'

Now we must admit that there is wrong somewhere when the mind and soul are not in a state of peace and happiness. Pain is the alarm-bell which tells us something is wrong. If all were perfectly right within us and about us, satisfaction and thankfulness would fill the spirit. But if we are dissatisfied and apprehensive and distressed, then there is something wrong; such a state has a sufficient cause. But suppose people who are restless and suffering mistake the cause of their trouble, suppose they think it comes from something from which it does not come, all their efforts to cure it will be useless. They will be trying to make a change somewhere where no change is needed or is possible, and they will leave the real cause of the mischief without interference to continue its disturbances.

Now it is certain that people who try to do God's will, who try to bring their souls into union with the will of God by prayer, and to carry out that will in daily life, are well-pleasing in the sight of God. In Bible words, they are *reconciled to God*. For reconciliation with God simply means taking God's will as ours, so that there is no discord between the two. Reconciliation with God can only mean union with God. He who takes God's will, as it becomes known to him, and makes it his own, is one with God, is reconciled to God. However dark or uncertain or apprehensive or distressed may be his spirit, that does not in the least interfere with his reconcilia-

SPIRITUAL DEPRESSION

tion with God, any more than the anguish of neuralgia shakes a man's credit with his banker. If a man's will is one with the will of God, that is reconciliation; and as long as his will is one with the will of God there can be no break in the reconciliation. If a man were to lie long on a bed of sickness, distressed and fearing lest his soul should be lost, and if he were to die and his last words were words of agitation and alarm, that would not in the very least interfere with his reconciliation, it would have nothing to do with it, any more than the vapours and fogs of earth can destroy the sun. Such a reconciled spirit, one with God like his suffering Saviour Christ, would pass in death from the earthly atmosphere of fog and vapour to the serener regions where the sun ever shines 'and there is no night there.'

But it is quite certain that many of these reconciled souls attribute their perplexities to a wrong cause; they think their sufferings prove that their hearts are not right in the sight of God. Whereas it often happens that their bodies are not right or their heads are not right. However we may explain the alliance between the body and the mind, the mind we know is influenced by the body. In certain diseases, mental depression is an invariable concomitant. Some people are born with a low tone. All their lives long they see, as we say, the dark side of things. They view everything through a gloomy medium. If they had never been taught any religion, nor ever heard about

God; or if from childhood they had been led to believe that God would in the long run rescue all His creatures from evil and pain, and that a hell of eternal sin was impossible unless the Devil were a God as powerful as the God of heaven; still, whatever the creed or no-creed, they would certainly take a sad, apprehensive view of things. Instead of putting this sad view down to its true cause—their bodily health or organic tone—they put it down to the anger of God, to the withholding of the light of His countenance, and employ prayers when tonics would be more useful. Such cases as these are very obstinate at times; they are a distressing perplexity to the minister of religion, who knows how little good can come from arguing with a man's constitution. You can tell such persons to be patient, and say that they may grow out of it, that constitutional changes may in time bring brightness to them, but that in the meanwhile they must be manly and uncomplaining, and bear their burden. They must remember that others too have burdens, it may be of poverty, or the infidelity of those who share their life, or the shame and pang of useless or worthless offspring, while they have a constitutional burden which they must bear,

With close-lipp'd patience for their only friend.[1]

And here comes in the secret of this good text: 'Let

[1] Mr. M. Arnold.

him trust in the name of the Lord, and stay upon his God.' Such an one can say, and should say, and labour at it until it becomes a great moral conquest, a bearing of the cross, 'This burden comes from my frail body, and not from a vacillating God, not from a Sovereign who turns away His head with disdain from some, and capriciously smiles upon a favourite. God is good, and God is wise; and I am in His great hands, and all shall be well if I only patiently and silently bear. Yes, silently bear, for then only one need suffer; but if I go about telling my ailments and ills, whether they be those of body or mind, I shall make others suffer as well as myself. I shall be a persecutor rather than a martyr.'

It may be that silence is gold, but eternally talking about silence being gold is scarcely pinchbeck. If silence commonly is gold, silence when we are worried and perplexed is more than gold, its price is above rubies. And it does distress us when we approach lofty genius, as we do in the lives of Carlyle and George Eliot, to be stunned by the constant bellowings of the one, and wearied with the monotonous complainings of the other. Alas! neither had in its fulness the faith of Christ in God. His faith was the faith of a Jewish poet, 'I was dumb and opened not my mouth, for it was thy doing,' and of a Jewish prophet, 'He is led as a lamb to the slaughter, and as a sheep before her shearers is dumb, so he openeth not his mouth.' Only in His last physical extremity was one cry of anguish wrung from the Spirit of Christ, 'My God, my God, why hast Thou forsaken me?' The triumph of Christianity over doubts engendered by disease can only come from a simple, manly confidence in the unchangeable goodness of God. To win this may be the life-discipline for some, and noble is the attainment when such in despondency can yet say, 'Though He slay me, yet will I put my trust in Him.' And so it is with many of the sorrows of life which bring a cloud upon our summer day. Why is it, we say? What good can come of it? Why am I left desolate? Is life worth living? Is not wickedness triumphant and worthlessness successful? It is at such times that trust in God brings relief, and staying upon God the power to wait and the power to be patient. And if the thought should arise in you, that you are not ready to die, it simply means, if you are doing your duty, that you are meant to live. If you abide faithful, the readiness to die will be given you when the time to die is near.

But, again, there are many, and especially in seasons of religious excitement, who are troubled and restless because they have not experienced something which some people profess to experience, because, as they say, they do not feel that they have been converted, they do not remember any time when they were converted. And people say to them, 'Ah! you do not know the truth, you have not found the Lord.' And they cry and weep, they listen to words of instruction, and again they cry for pardon and hearken for a voice from heaven, and no voice seems to come. Now in many such cases no conversion whatever is needed. Already the life is simply and carefully ordered in the way of God's commandments; there is a desire to do good to others and to be a sweetness and strength at home. If you convert such a character you must make it bad, for conversion is turning a thing round into an opposite direction. Such people have not to be converted, they have to go straight on; or, if they have been only going slowly, then they must 'run the way set before them,' they must 'go on their way rejoicing.' But the disturbing teacher comes and tells them that because they do not know anything about a conversion, they are in the gall of bitterness and the bond of iniquity. He quotes verses which they cannot answer, verses which speak of being converted and believing on the Lord Jesus Christ, verses which had such a clear and direct meaning when they were addressed to heathens and Jews, but which cannot have the same meaning in reference to those who have believed in Christ from their childhood and walked in the paths of virtue from their earliest days. Nevertheless they are distressed and alarmed by this irrational earnestness. A preacher[1] of this school of irrational earnestness says, there is a class of persons which 'has usually its representatives in our morning

---

[1] Rev. W. H. Aitken.

congregations'—I wonder where they go at night, or do they only go once a day to church?—and he says, 'This class consists of those who are leading outwardly decent, respectable, and even religious lives.' He does not hint, when he uses the word *outwardly*, that perhaps in secret they are bad and indecent and irreligious, he clearly means that their lives *are* decent, respectable, and religious, for if it were not so they would be hypocrites, and would not be the people referred to. He means—or else the passage is without meaning — really decent, respectable, religious people; for a man who is outwardly decent, respectable, and religious, and is not so inwardly, is simply a cheat, an impostor. Now he says, what I cannot agree with, that this class 'found in our morning congregations,' leading 'decent and respectable and even religious lives, and who attend church regularly,' may be 'without any personal experience of the justifying grace of God.' I should say that that is simply impossible. Justifying grace is the grace which makes a man just, the grace which puts him into his right place, which makes his will one with God, reconciles him to God. It is the grace which makes him decent, respectable, and religious. He whose life is in accordance with the will of God does possess this justifying grace; it has wrought its effects in him; 'every good gift and every perfect gift is from above—by their fruits shall ye know them.' Do not allow your minds to be harassed and disturbed by irrationality, however earnest. It may be that even to-day the words of the prophet Ezekiel may be applicable to some, 'Because with lies ye have made the heart of the righteous sad whom I have not made sad.' But we are sad, say you; this teaching has laid hold of us; we must go on our way, but we cannot go on our way rejoicing. And why not? Is not God your Father and Friend? Is not Christ your redeeming, saving Brother? Does not the Spirit bid you say Father? All this is true, true as heaven and earth, and truer, for they shall perish. But may I really be sure that God is my Father, and may I say it and believe it and hold it fast? Yes, indeed; say it *now* and press it to your heart, and never let a doubt arise upon it. Be sure that while you live seeking the will of God in all things, and praying daily that it may more and more abide in you, be sure that you are the child of God, every day be sure about it. Be sure, when sickness or sorrow or shame or ruin befall you, that you are the child of God; and when your last breath rises to your lips with the flitting spirit, let its last word be 'Father.'

XIV.

'DEVOTIONALITY.'

'Stablish Thy word unto Thy servant, who is devoted to Thy fear.'—*Psalm* cxix. 38.

INSISTING, as I ever do, that religion rests upon a foundation as solid and as positive as that upon which physical science is built—the existence of God and the existence of Nature being alike affirmations of the human mind, ultimate, or in other words dogmatic—piety is the response which the soul spontaneously makes when this great reality is perceived. Religious emotion, '*effusion*,' addressed to the Great Unbounded Nothing, I do not understand. It is as rational as the gas which escapes from a balloon, dissipating into the empty infinite. But if religious emotion is only rational when it is evoked by some sufficient reality, so also I am unable to conceive a religion whose essence is not devotion. It never occurred to me that any one might think a devout temper of mind undesirable. It has always seemed to me that certain emotions were the natural response to certain objects, and that, in the presence of God, devotion was not only appropriate but inevitable, and that it was well that the loftiest feeling a man was capable of should tinge his whole activity. Indeed, I should have been disposed to say, that every man with a heart must feel a kind of devotion to something—if not to the highest, then to something lower; that to be incapable of devotion is to be without a heart, and to be without a heart is to be an evil spirit; or, to use the figurative words of the Bible, to be a child of the Devil. The highest expression of devotion we call worship, and its great opportunity is the general assembly of the Church. But there is a saying of Arthur Clough, on which by accident I lighted, which made me look at these thoughts of mine and reconsider them, and which in a minute I will quote, but with which the more I think of it, the more I disagree If it be true, then I cannot conceive the utility of public worship, nor of private worship either; nor of that tender overflow of the spirit of worship we call devotion on the whole life; nor, indeed, the possibility of any worship at all. For I suppose we none of us think that by certain regulated formalities and ecclesiastical machinery we can manipulate the heavenly world, as the sails of a mill are managed from below. We do not think we come to church to work upon the Almighty by a prescribed ritual; nor, by a kind of celestial wizardry, to make heavenly spirits do our bidding. We do not think we come here to alter the mind and law of God, which are holy and just and good. It is to express our own minds and souls, and to alter our own minds and souls, we come here to draw nigh to God. But if we do not attain to worship, and if worship is not to be aimed at, and is undesirable, then I think some use should be found for the churches. They are utterly wasted now. If they are only lecture-halls and music-halls, then we have enough without them and better than they. The lectures at the Royal Institution are better than the generality of sermons, they are more various and interesting. *We* are confined to a limited region of topics—*there* the study is the world. If we want the finest music, then, as a rule, Monday will become the sacred day rather than Sunday. And even if the church music and the church lecture be of the best, they are spoiled, if there be no real worship, by wearisome, unmeaning, and unprofitable prayers. The one thing I wish my preaching and our singing to do for you is, to help you to go up to the high altar of worship, there to sprinkle the incense that it may ascend in fragrant sacrifice. If I do this for you, then I need not be cast down because I am less various and eloquent and interesting than the popular lecturer, or because our music is that of simple psalm and hymn, and not that of the Mass, the oratorio, or the opera. But this is the saying of Clough to which I take exception, and I quote it because it may represent the conclusion of more minds than the writer's. 'The belief that religion is, or in any way requires, devotionality, is, if not the most noxious, at least the most obstinate, form of irreligion.'

The question arises, What is meant by *devotionality*? We should most of us be disposed to say, a devotional spirit and tone of mind. But surely a devotional spirit is not only appropriate, and in accordance with the fitness of things, but also the highest, in quality, of our various emotions. Mr. Clough has said, in the very same essay, 'Our faith must not rest on historical facts, however strongly attested, not on theological articles, however ancient and venerable, not on any written *semper ubique ab omnibus*, but on the instincts of the spiritual sense, the demands of the spiritual nature.' But with what must the spiritual senses be employed? Why, with that which is spiritual, with that which cannot be seen by mortal eye, with the things unseen which are eternal. It is the sense by which, to use the Bible words, we see God. And if the spiritual sense sees God, what does the spiritual nature demand when God is seen? That we bow down in solemn, delighted, yet adoring awe. The only emotion which is appropriate, rational, I may say natural, when the Mighty Presence of whom are all things is revealed—a Presence which is greater than Humanity, vaster than the universe, holding all things together in unity, yet without and beyond and above and around all things in limitless sweep, the infinite, everlasting, omnipresent mind—is awe. When that Presence is brought still nearer to us in a saving form, and through Christ we find a loving, pardoning, heavenly Father, the only emotion possible is adoring, confiding reverence. Is this devotionality? Then a man who is incapable of it is less than a boor, he is a clod—to quote a verse of the same writer,

> Neither man's aristocracy this nor God's, God knoweth.

One may well say, 'Better not be at all than not be noble.'

But it is possible that by devotionality may be meant the neglect of practical life for absorption in Divine contemplation. For the writer speaks of devotionality as more common in Roman Catholic countries than in England. He talks of absorption in the contemplation of the Deity being the whole life. Now that this is to be condemned is evident. For he who neglects his worldly duties is as imperfect and one-sided as he who does not respond to his heavenly environment. The world is a fact as God Himself is a fact, and we must respond appropriately to each. We are not only religious beings, but social beings; and if we are to be perfect, we must be all that we are capable of being, we must live all round, live our complete lives. The patriot is not to ignore his family, the intellectual man his body, nor any his soul. It is true that absorption in religion, while the other relationships of life are ignored, is perverting and mutilating. For a human being to live an exclusively religious life is to be half dead; as it is to be half dead to lead a merely worldly life. But is there much danger of our leading a life of absorption in religion? There may be more danger of it in Catholic countries. The cloister has constrained many to find in spiritual raptures, reached by asceticism, the joys denied them elsewhere. But is this a danger against which the generality of Englishmen need to be particularly guarded? Are you afraid, you men of high position and active profession and crowded affairs, that you are really in danger of becoming too religious? Do you feel that you need plucking up from your knees, lest you should forget to go down to the House, or to be in Court, or Chambers, or society, because you are absorbed in devotion? Do you think you will lose many fees, or dinners, or dances, because you are so entranced by heavenly ecstacy that the world is an alien and forgotten thing? —while

> deep asleep he seem'd, yet all awake,
> And music in his ears his beating heart did make.

No, that is not the danger. The danger which most of us feel, which drives some of us to church on Sundays, that perchance we may escape it, is that of absorption in the world and destitution in religion. The danger is the hurrying life of business or of society—dressing and dining, talking about the same things until we are tired to death of them, and pushing into new places which soon become as monotonous as the old, working and worrying year after year, trying to look young when unkind age is scoring his lines upon us; and still each year coming back to the same dull round of work and pleasure, ever growing duller, until men shake their heads over us and say—'He is gone,' having lived without God in the world. I know you are not afraid of becoming too prayerful. There is no need to guard you against an encroaching devotionality. I would we had a little more of this Catholic spirit. It is a rational spirit and a becoming spirit. It is the only reasonable response to the greatest of facts. Other facts we must also respond to. But I venture to think that devotionality will add new energy and warmth to sociality.

Why, even science herself encourages a kind of devotionality; and we can see the reason and the necessity for it, in cases where God is ignored. Then Nature or Humanity becomes the highest thought and presence, and to that which is highest, the mind is constrained to pay its homage. Take these words of the late Professor Clifford on the nature of 'Cosmic emotion,' and do they not implicitly contain the essence of devotionality—unless you prefer to describe them as 'poetic religiosity'? He says, 'When we try to put together the most general conceptions that we can form about the great aggregate of events that are always going on, to strike a sort of balance among the feelings which these events produce in us, and to add to these the feeling of vastness associated with an attempt to represent the whole of existence, then we experience a cosmic emotion—which may have the character of awe, veneration, resignation, submission.' Or take these words of the author of the book called 'Natural Religion.' 'It is true,' he says, 'that the scientific man cannot feel for Nature such love as a pious mind may feel for the God of Christians. The highest love is inspired by love, or by justice and goodness, and of these qualities science as yet discovers little or nothing in Nature. . . . This arresting, absorbing spectacle, so fascinating by its variety, is at the same time overwhelming by its greatness; so that those who have devoted their lives to the contemplation scarcely ever fail to testify to the endless delight it gives them, and also to the overpowering awe with which, from time to time, it surprises them.' Or, again, take the following words of Comte, for whom Humanity is the Great Being, the highest thought, the object of adoration. He says, 'Next to the practice of good deeds, nothing tends more to develop the sympathetic instincts than due expression of the emotions as a familiar use.' That expression he tells us is prayer. 'To pray,' he says, 'is to love and to think in one;' 'Prayer in its purest form offers the best type of life, and conversely life in its noblest aspect consists in one long prayer.' These are the very words of Comte; it is the founder of Positivism pleading for devotionality. Or take the words of a Deist overflowing with devotionality. 'The single thought, "God is for my soul, and my soul is for Him," suffices to fill a universe of feeling. Spiritual persons have exhausted human relationships in the vain attempt to express their full sense of what God (or Christ) is to them.'[1]

It is clear that the devotional temper is necessary to all who can perceive greatness. Take an illustration of what I mean from one of our most engrossing emotions, the emotion of love. True it is a warmer, more corporeal feeling than that of devotion or worship. But love, without the movings of tenderness, admiration and delight towards the beloved object, would be just as natural as religion without devotion. And here let me say that those who remember or retain the emotion of *devoted* love, can tell how it tinged the day with its brightness, or now shines down upon it a happy content; it gave new hope and new energy to life, it gave happiness, and happiness can always do the best work. The joy of love has made men first-rate, it has at times put a new fervency and gratitude into their prayers. It may collapse into maudlin fondness and unbraced languishment. Everything is liable to disease. But a healthy body is not to be despised because you may poison it. And just so it is with true devotion. It has its rare moments of intuition, of spiritual delight. But these moments shed a refreshing dew on all the life,

<blockquote>And touch the apathetic ghosts with joy.</blockquote>

Mr. Matthew Arnold has said, 'The true meaning

[1] Mr. F. Newman.

of religion is not simply morality, but morality touched by emotion.' And he calls this touching of morality by emotion 'the elevation and inspiration of morality.' There is much I agree with in this. But I would rather reverse the sentence. For the essence of religion is not morality. Religion arises from our relationship to God, morality arises from a social condition. 'What is religion but the system of relationships existing between us and a supreme being?'[1] Even if there were no God, some sort of morality must exist or society would perish. Therefore I would not quite say that 'religion is morality touched by emotion.' Rather would I say, religion is emotion touching morality and the whole life, emotion inspiring morality, and so giving it new sanction and new energy. It is devotion, casting upon life a radiance which comes from God.

[1] Newman.

XV.

THE CALLS OF GOD.

'Now the Lord had said unto Abram, Get thee out of thy country, and from thy kindred, and from thy father's house, unto a land that I will shew thee: and I will make of thee a great nation, and I will bless thee, and make thy name great; and thou shalt be a blessing: and I will bless them that bless thee, and curse him that curseth thee: and in thee shall all families of the earth be blessed. So Abram departed, as the Lord had spoken unto him.'—*Genesis* xii. 1-4.

THIS is the account of what is named the 'Call of Abraham.' It not only shows us the way in which the Jewish people, long centuries afterwards, believed that their nation had started on its course—and that which a nation believes about its own history must always be acting on its character, whether it be fact or fable, and noble traditions make noble races—but these words, containing the story of Abraham's call, point distinctly to a nucleus of positive history. Although Dr. Kuenen, the learned Professor of the University of Leyden, says that 'the narratives of Genesis are founded upon a theory of the origin of nations which the historical science of the present day rejects without the slightest hesitation,' and that the patriarchs 'as progenitors of tribes are but personifications,' he yet asks, 'What should hinder us from assuming that some centuries before Israel settled in Canaan, a mighty shepherd prince named Abraham had set up his tents near Hebron?' Ewald more confidently declares that 'he who could still doubt the reality of the lives of Abraham and Lot can scarcely be even beginning to see anything with certainty in this field of history.'

The certainties for us are, that a family or small tribe migrated from Mesopotamia into Palestine, whose head or sheik was Abraham; that the impulse which moved it from its original dwelling-place was religious; and that from this family or tribe, powerful enough to engage in wars and form equal alliances with the kinglets of Palestina, the Jewish nation arose; that that which governed the small tribe became eventually the bond of a nation, a bond so strong that Egypt and Assyria, and Babylonia and Greece, and Rome and all the wrenchings of the modern nations have been unable to force it away—and that bond was religion. The religious spirit and genius, which moved the Abrahamic nomads, was inherited and augmented by their descendants, and has never been equalled, as yet, by any race of mankind. And that is the reason why we Western Aryans still turn to Semitic history for our religious teaching. Apart from religion, Jewish history is a less profitable, certainly a less interesting, subject of study than English history. Of themselves, Alfred and Harold are more to us than Saul and

Ahab; and the Reformation of Henry more touching than that of Jehu or of Josiah. But you cannot rid the Bible of religion. The history is steeped in religion. Its whole attitude is that of no other history. Its explanation is singular. Its power is undying. In a word, it is inspired. And so I am going to speak on the Call of Abraham because of its inspiration; and we shall find that it is a picture of God's method of dealing with each one of us.

For I am sure that, at some time in our lives, a call from God sends its trumpet tone through each of our souls, as it did when Abraham heard it, and he went forth with the future stretching broad and far before him, empty now, and yet to be filled by his ever-increasing offspring. From what did God call Abraham, and to what did He call him? It is said that God called him from his kindred and from his father's house; and, in doing so, we know that God called him into closer communion with Himself. The great fact about Abraham, which has stamped itself upon the minds of countless generations, is his religiousness—in Bible words, that he was 'the friend of God.' To this moment the town near which he dwelt so long, and where tradition unquestioned has fixed his burial-place—Hebron—is called El Khalil, the Friend. We have no reason to believe that Abraham's knowledge of God was as pure and clear as that of the later prophets; but it was a step forward, and a very large one, in the evolution of Divine revelation, or it could not have made the lasting impression it has done. Remember, Abraham came out of what we should call a heathen or polytheistic home. Tradition says that his father was a maker of idols; and the words of Joshua prove his heathen origin, 'Thus saith the Lord God of Israel, your fathers dwelt on the other side of the flood in old time, even Terah, the father of Abraham, and the father of Nachor; and they served other gods. And I took your father Abraham from the other side of the flood.' His descendants for many generations were infected with idol worship. The kindred nations around them remained idolaters. Only by a slow process of ascension were higher views of God attained.

In olden times men were much in the habit of regarding the state of things which they saw around them as a fall from a purer primitive condition. We, in these days, rather think of a Divine education, leading man upward as he is able to bear it; of a continuous ascension, with heaven as the summit. The inspiration of Abraham, in this respect, was modern, and his face was to the future. But how long is prophecy before it is fulfilled! Great thoughts are uttered, but it takes ages to assimilate them, so that they become part of the mental tissue of a whole nation or age. Take, for instance, the condemnation of human sacrifice implied in the offering up of Isaac. Human sacrifice could scarcely have been unfamiliar to the mind of Abraham; for when the voice, which is to him Divine, bids him slay his son, he does not appear to be disturbed by surprise, or moved to remonstrance, or smitten with a great horror. We cannot put it to ourselves what we should think, if we believed we were commanded by God to commit murder. If we could think at all at such a frightful moment, we should rush away to some one who could hold us back from a deed of irresponsible insanity. If even the impression seized upon us, for an instant, that it was God's will we should kill our child, if we fancied that we heard a Divine voice calling upon us to kill our child, we should feel that we were going mad, and we should fly to others to save us from the terrible danger.

But Abraham was not without a sense of the moral character of God. When the destruction of Sodom and Gomorrah was made known to him, and the thought that the righteous and the wicked were to be involved in one undiscriminating doom was presented to him, his moral nature did rise up in protest. The protest of his soul against what seemed injustice was, 'That be far from Thee that the righteous should be as the wicked. Shall not the Judge of all the earth do right?' But, as I have said, he uttered no cry nor remonstrance when the command to slay his son was forced upon him, as though some unheard-of, horrible thing had happened to him. The absolute right of the Divine Being to the lives of His creatures must have been with him an ingrained conviction. And it was a new revelation, a new inspiration, a new starting-place in the history of religion, an epoch to be had in everlasting remembrance, when the voice, like the voice of discovery, sounded in his soul, 'Lay not thine hand upon the lad, neither do thou anything unto him.' This was indeed the voice of God. It was a new commandment which in fact bade him and his descendants take the animal for sacrifice instead of the man, until the perfect idea of sacrifice should be revealed, and the summit of revelation reached by Christ, who came to put away sin by the sacrifice of Himself.

But how long, notwithstanding this great revelation made to Abraham, human sacrifice lingered on, even among his descendants, we all know. The daughter of Jephthah and the hewing of Agag in pieces 'before the Lord' are instant recollections. The redemption of the firstborn seems to point to it; and the custom burst forth again after it had been for a while suppressed, stirred into activity by the neighbouring races, in the times of some of the later kings, who made sons and daughters to 'pass through the fire.' It has been said, 'Ordinary men see the fruits of their action; the seed sown by men of genius germinates slowly.'[1] And it is just as true of that specially Divine genius which we name inspiration, or Divine revelation through the mind of man.

[1] Mommsen.

How God called Abraham we are not told. We rather incline to fancy that, in old Bible days, God called people in a different way from that in which He calls them now, instead of perceiving that the only difference is the difference in the way of expressing the fact. We materialise the poetry of Eastern expression until we are in danger of forgetting that God is the same yesterday and to-day and for ever; and that it was as true in the far-off past, and in the tent of the nomad chieftain, as it is to-day in the crowded city and in the kneeling church, that 'God is a Spirit,' and that 'no man hath seen God at any time.' Such sayings as that 'God talked face to face,' and that 'Abraham stood yet before the Lord,' cannot for one moment change the nature of the Eternal whom 'no man hath seen or can see.' We may forget it, but God is as really seen by the intuition of faith in the soul, as He would be were men's senses overwhelmed by an unspeakable mystery, and His voice is as Divine when it is heard in the reason and in the conscience, as when it thunders through the sky.

In whatever way God called Abraham, it was a call to his soul. In whatever way the call came, all must admit that its purpose was to reach his soul. It made him begin to question the truth of the religion in which he had been brought up; it forced him to see the gods and the worship of his fathers and of his home in a new and painful light. It drew him away in thought and view from those who were nearest and dearest to him. It called him to think, and think thoroughly and understand, whether the gods of the earth and the gods of the seas and the gods of the skies were still to have his worship; or the God who, he believed, had spoken to him and beckoned him away. He must have suffered from long and lonely and painful thought. The past does not loose its hold upon us easily. The doubt arises, when we feel called to take a new step, a different work, a strange and unwelcome position—

> The tremor that intrudes
> When firmest seems our faith [1]—

'May I not be mistaken, am I not excited, did I really hear what I thought I heard, did I really see what I thought I saw? If I am right, then my father and mother and relations, and the wise and good who have lived before me, have all been in error. Is it not more likely that I should have made a mistake than that so many, better than I, should be wrong? Is it not presumptuous in me to doubt what so many wise and holy people believed through life and in death?' And still the voice of God, like a hand, keeps beckoning away, and, for awhile, a man is joyless and irresolute. His mind is not made up. He dare not tell the doubts which consume him, for his friends will be horrified. He will inflict bitter pain on those who care for him and believe in him,

[1] Mr. Browning.

but who know not, and who cannot hear the voice which keeps speaking to him.

God's call to a man is always, at first, a call into loneliness. For, in the hum and chatter and profitless jingle of common life, a man called of God cannot stay. Through it all he hears the solemn tolling call, and he must be up and away and come to the life or death decision. So doubtless was it with Abraham. His old forms of worship and religious symbols would become tiresome to him, unreal, untrue. He perhaps tried for awhile to put new and higher meanings into them, to see them in the light of a new idea; but a man cannot live in illusions long. The cry of the soul is for reality. 'Let me be sure, let me be honest, let me be true; for I cannot live and seem to be that which indeed I am not. I must arise and go forth into the lonely ways of life, for a voice is calling me which I cannot disobey. Day and night a magnet is drawing me, and though I stand still and ponder and hesitate, yet I know how it will all end. Bitter as is the pang of separation, and hard as it is to seem to be a traitor and renegade in the eyes which have beamed in tenderness upon me, yet I must hurry away; for the voice keeps sounding which will not let me stop, and the attraction is drawing which will not let me stand, and I must arise and depart, for this is not my rest.' So must it have been with Abraham, the father of the faithful. Human nature alters but little essentially, and each man's own experience tells the tale of duty and its first reward, loneliness and pain. 'So Abram departed as the Lord had spoken unto him.'

Here, then, we may leave our little study of the Call of Abraham. But of this I am sure, that until we can be manly and true enough to follow the voice of God, as it sounds in our consciences and in our souls, into loneliness—away from common men, with their common aims and common hopes and common pleasures—until we can dare to cut the cords which bind us by nature to those whose lives and faith we can in truth no longer share, there is no great salvation for us. It is quite certain that God has spoken at some time to every one of us. In your soul the voice Divine has sounded. It may have come to you in church. It made you tremble, and you almost said, 'I will arise.' It may have come to you in sickness, or when death just looked at you, and in his stony gaze your heart near stopped for chillness. It may have come to you in hours of bitter pain and sorrow, in hours when you waited for some terrible stroke. It may have come to you by the grave of one you tenderly loved. In many ways it may have come. It bade you leave that sin which is your disgrace and misery. It bade you forsake those companions whose influence degraded you, and made you harder and coarser and less reverent and less religious. It bade you rise above that decent conformity to religious services—a worship which is but a passionless performance and a reverent absence of mind—and cease to act the play of a once living religion. It may have called you to think for yourself, to follow a truth which has arisen like a guiding star upon you. It may have told you to take your place as a man of God and a worker for God. It may have called you to wear upon your brow the stamp and seal of heaven. Oh! one cannot tell to what degree of singular eminence that voice of God may not have called some of us, who may now be tame as a desert flat, and unimpassioned as ashes. And I know why so many of us, who are good and honourable men, never become men of great use, and example, and higher thought and true devotion. We dare not be singular. We dare not leave our kindred nor our set. We will not leave our traditional views and sentiments, and we cannot leave our secret sins. Other voices have more power over us than the voice of the Almighty. Pleasure speaks, and we say, I come. And greed speaks, and we say, I come. Ambition speaks, and we say, I come. And God speaks, and we close our eyes, and turn away our heads, and our coward hearts give back the response they dare not clothe in words, I will not come. How long will all this last? Will it last until another solemn voice shall speak to us, and at the call of death we say, I come?

Printed by Spottiswoode & Co., New-street Square, London.

www.ingramcontent.com/pod-product-compliance
Lightning Source LLC
Chambersburg PA
CBHW020925230426
43666CB00008B/1573